# 101 BATTLE TESTED P/R STRATEGIES FOR SUCCESSFUL FUNERAL DIRECTORS

# 101 BATTLE TESTED P/R STRATEGIES FOR SUCCESSFUL FUNERAL DIRECTORS

Introducing a Powerful New P/R Strategy

THOMAS ANONYMOUS

Copyright © 2019 by Thomas Anonymous.

ISBN    Softcover    978-1-951469-88-7

All rights reserved. No part of this book may be reproduced or transmitted in any form or by any means, electronic or mechanical, including photocopying, recording, or by any information storage and retrieval system without express written permission from the author, except in the case of brief quotations embodied in critical reviews and certain other non-commercial uses permitted by copyright law.

Printed in the United States of America.

To order additional copies of this book, contact:
Bookwhip
1-855-339-3589
www.bookwhip.com

# Index

**INTRODUCTION** ........................................................... vii

**1. MY BOSS'S WIFE'S' DOG** ......................................... 1
Pay Attention To The Little Things That Can "Bite" You

**2. GOLD NUGGETS** ....................................................... 6
Become A Prospector

**3. YOUR HERD OF CONTENTED COWS** ....................... 11
Ways To keep Them Contented

**4. LET UNCLE SAM CARRY THE LOAD** ....................... 37
Give Your P/R A Boost By Mail

**5. YOUR BIG GUNS** ..................................................... 49
Battle-Tested And Ready For Action

**6. A GLANCE AT YOUR SECRET WEAPON** .................. 64
Your Comprehensive Five Pronged Program

**7. A CRASH COURSE IN GRIEF RECOVERY** ................ 72
Book Section

# 1
## INTRODUCTION

# ARE YOU IN A LIFE OR DEATH BATTLE FOR SURVIVAL?

Have you ever stood on the seashore just after a violent storm, and observed the crashing waves? In some areas, beaches are littered with wreckage of ships, and we shudder at their destruction. A mile or so down the beach, others may be standing on the edge of the water, with their surf boards, waiting for the next wave to recede, so they can follow it out, and ride the next one in. On one hand, disaster, on the other opportunity.

How do funeral service professionals view this economic storm? Do they wonder how their funeral home can stay afloat in these turbulent economic waters, or go under like the Titanic. Funeral directors are experts at weathering economic typhoons and tornadoes. In my lifetime, I have seen them survive three major disasters, and come out better because of them.

My grandfather, an old time undertaker, operated out of a store front office, and embalmed bodies in peoples' homes. A sharp competitor almost put him out of business by opening the first *"funeral home"* in the area. People loved the concept, and you know the rest of the story.

The Federal Government threw the funeral industry a curve ball when they imposed Federal Trade Commission (FTC), and Occupational Safety (OSHA) "rules" on the industry. It was a blessing in disguise, because it forced many sleazy operators to be honest. Most of us have weathered the telemarketing storm, along with direct disposal companies and storefront casket outlets. Can you imagine anyone in funeral service today operating without a computer or website?

I've read about survival at sea in ancient days. The first thing they did was to lighten the load of the ship. They threw everything that was excessive weight, including the cargo, overboard. Think long and hard before you throw good people overboard, in this economic Tsunami. Consider asking every one of your staff to take a cut in pay so no one has to be tossed overboard.

I've noticed that some funeral homes and many other businesses increase their advertising when things slow down. *Don't do it.* In my opinion, advertising is the first place to cut if things get tight. I'll get into that in more detail later.

## Wonderful Opportunity

Funeral directors are standing on the shores of a vast expanse of untapped opportunity. This program will allow the funeral home, as we know it, to transition to the funeral home of the future, which I call the "Grief Recovery Resource Center." The concept is explained in the funeral home section of "A Crash Course In Grief Recovery," in the last section of this book. It will require very little investment. It is not difficult to grasp, and it's not complicated. It will require some extra time to master the concepts at first, and a burning desire to help people get rid of the awful load of grief so many are carrying around with them. Compared to the hours you have spent mastering your computer, it'll be a "piece of cake."

I know the first thought you're going to have. "I'm in a life or death battle for survival, right now, and I don't want anything new or costly to deal with." Hold on a minute, my friend. You can't measure satisfaction, or contentment. I can guarantee that if you stick with this program, you'll be both contented and satisfied. The economy will determine how prosperous you become.

## Goliath

When I think of life or death battles, it reminds me of David and Goliath. You remember, in the Bible (1 Samuel, chapter 17). A shepherd boy entered into life or death combat with a giant and won. The giant was about ten feet tall, had the most sophisticated weaponry and armor of his time, and was backed by the fiercest army in the world. However, the giant had vulnerabilities, and David seized on them. He used the element of surprise, a secret weapon, and brought Goliath crashing to the ground.

## You, Too, Can Be Victorious Over Your Goliaths

Obviously, the giant did not expect the teenage boy to rush him, or use a sling shot as a weapon of war. Just as Goliath had left himself wide open to David's flying projectile, your competitors won't expect what you're going to throw at them, either.

You know that one well planned P/R strategy can give you a decided edge over your competition. Here are over one hundred of them, battle-tested and ready to deploy. I invite you to apply them as you transition into the future. We used many of these strategies to propel our little firm, in a bedroom community, doing fifty some odd calls a year, in a fiercely competitive struggle against seven top-flight funeral homes and a branch facility. When my business partner and I retired, we were doing over two hundred calls a year.

Change has never been easy. Remember, unless we go through the storm, and experience the difficulties, we probably will not appreciate the blessings when they arrive. Funeral service professionals are on "center stage" in the drama of life. Play your part to perfection.

Someone told my wife about the services for a baby. The funeral director was carrying the child in it's casket from the funeral home to the car, shoulder level, balanced on the palm of his hand, like a pizza delivery boy. Remember, someone's lifetime impression of you may be made in a few moments.

## Your Actions Speak So Loud, They Can't Hear What You Say!

*"They Were SO Nice To Me,"* my wife exclaimed, on her recent return from a trip to the grocery store. "That clerk went out of her way to help me!" My wife is not going to forget that for a long time. The clerk, hopefully, will move on to much better things, but my wife's lasting impression will be with that store.

A friend of mine has a very prosperous trash removal service. "I'll bet at Christmas time I get three times as many tips as my other drivers do, because I take time to be sure the covers are securely placed on the containers, after they are emptied. I put them so they are not going to blow out in the road if it's windy, and I pick up around them if anything has spilled over." *It's The Little Things That Make The Difference! People instinctively know if your heart is in it.*

*\*\* Do people see your men with their shoes shined, and a necktie?* Do they see your female employees with attractive(not seductive)clothing? Are your men's hair cut? Pants pressed? Do the women have pierced noses and lips? Do they wear appropriate earrings? There should be no question in anyone's mind as to what is acceptable and what is not!

---

### Our Attitude Is Infectious

Directing a funeral, for us, is an everyday thing. To most people, especially the family, it's the biggest thing in their lives right now, and <u>extremely</u> important to them! They dwell on it, and go over the details again and again in their conversations with family and friends for years to come. To many people it's a solemn ritual. Give every person, and every detail, maximum respect and dignity. People only see us for a few minutes, and the impression we leave is ingrained in their memory for the rest of their lives.

---

# CHAPTER 1

# MY BOSS'S WIFE'S' DOG

## Pay Attention To The Little Things That Can Bite You

I want to tell you about my boss' wife's dog. It was just a mean spirited little mutt. That thing clung closer to her than her shadow. Every time it came into the room where I was, it bared it's teeth and growled at me.

One day the boss' wife unexpectedly passed me something. Like lightning, that cur darted out from behind the lady and sank it's fangs into my leg. Then it ran back and hid behind her skirt. For years I resented that mutt. Then, it struck me like a ton of bricks. It was my own darned fault that dog bit me. I could have paid a little more attention to her and made friends with her.

It took a dog bite to wake me up, but when I finally came to, I realized that there were many wonderful P/R opportunities, right under my nose. Like with that dog, I had chosen to not pay attention to them. For example, most funeral homes probably throw away a ton of flowers every year. There are a number of ways flowers can be used to one's P/R advantage.

## Thomas Anonymous

In the Crash Course In Grief Recovery section of this book, I talk about a widowed persons support group that would probably enjoy taking vases of flowers apart, sorting them out, and making little vases of them, for nursing homes, shut-ins, soup kitchens, day care centers, and even local businesses. Speaking of flowers, I'm sure you video tape each arrangement and include it on the video of the service for each family. This is especially nice for folks who have sent flowers by "wire". People will grumble sometimes that they spent a lot more for flowers that were sent, than the value of what was delivered reflected.

*Want to improve the appearance of your floral arrangements by a thousand percent? It will cost a few dollars, but your return on investment will be well worth it. Find a piece of velvet from an old dress or something. Cut it round, about the size of a dinner plate. Lay it evenly over one of your metal flower racks, then set a vase of flowers on it. Now imagine your whole display of flowers with the "dress-ups" under all the vases. Classy, or what? The better the quality of the velvet, the easier they will be to keep looking spiffy. They will wrinkle less and last longer, though they will need to be hemmed. You're welcome. You may have to go to a thrift shop to find an old velvet dress.*

Most florists took time to make a note on the back of the cards telling folks what the arrangement was. If they didn't, we did.

There is a sense of serenity and well being when one walks into a room with a well balanced flower display. Here are a few tips to make your displays more "balanced": You already place close family arrangements near the head of the casket. I tried to balance the other end of the casket with similarly colored arrangements. I tried to keep brightly colored arrangements near the floor. I drew an imaginary line just below the top of the casket, and tried to keep the larger, brighter arrangements below that line. The lighter colored pastels, etc. I would place at the top of the display. If there was a dark or brightly colored arrangement, I would try to place it knee-high at one end of the casket, balanced with a similar arrangement on the other end. I usually placed one large arrangement in the center, on the floor, in front of the casket. I tried to make groups of flowers off to the sides of the display, and really special arrangements, on a separate stand or table, to emphasize their uniqueness. I usually could find a delicate vase of roses, or something similar, to place near the guest book at the back of the church or funeral home. Yes, we used the same guest book.

At one point, during the time they were at the funeral home alone, I asked each family if there were any flowers they wanted me to change and if there were special ones that they wanted near the casket. This sometimes led to interesting displays. One time a family spent the good part of an afternoon rearranging my display. They were satisfied, because they all participated in the arrangement process. There was also a special bonding that developed between that family and me.

I got a chuckle one day, while arranging flowers. We paper clipped cards from the flowers to the ribbons so they could be spotted easily. Someone had bought me a silver tie clasp in the form of a paperclip. One day I was arranging flowers with a family watching. One woman very emphatically said to me, "Mr. Lord, I'll BUY you a nice tie clasp!"

This is a good place to remind you, never underestimate the talent of your florist. We were blessed with one of exceptional ability. She once made a scale model of a snowmobile, after a man died while driving one. Several times she made floral arrangements of trucks, when a trucker had died. Several times she made arrangements in the shape of a horseshoe.

Frequently she used unique pieces of wood, tiny trees and things she had found in the woods. When one young hunter died, she used taxidermied animals to build a woodsy floral display around. The point is, if you are serving a family whose loved one had a particular interest, convey that interest to the family's florist, with the family's approval.

Why not take your florists(one at a time)to lunch, and explain the "life appreciation" concept to them.(Try the same thing with your clergy, cemetery superintendent, every new business owner in town, and, as a bonus, try getting a few non-competitive business owners together for breakfast once a week.) You and your families may both may be pleasantly surprised.

One of the things I used to listen to floral delivery people yak about, was that funeral homes often restricted the times florists could deliver. Remember that anyone who despises you for such unnecessary irritations is the person who is going to tell everyone in their family, friends, and other people who could be your future clients! Just because the arrangement was delivered didn't mean it had to be put up at that moment. If florists were directed to deliver to a back door to which they had a key so it could remain locked, they could deliver at their convenience. The funeral home might consider an inside closed room with an inside door, locked from the other side as well. It might be wise to place a small air conditioner or space heater there to assure the freshness of the flowers.

I had a personal appreciation of flowers, when some were given to my wife one day, shortly after I went to work for a new company. It was a cold dreary day in late fall. My very pregnant wife was home alone with the kids, when a knock came at the door. It was my new boss, with a vase of fresh roses in his hand. He gave them to my wife, and introduced himself. He told my wife he was glad I had come to work for the company, and told her he hoped she would be happy there. Let me tell you friend, that boss could do no wrong in my wife's eyes from that day on!

I mentioned that we learned many things by trial and error. Here's one of our most notorious errors. My business partner and I threw away thousands of dollars worth of good will (P/R) because we thought it was too much bother to get up off our duffs once in a while and put a few folding chairs in the family's car for use at their home. Many of these public relations strategies have been developed because, like that dog, they snuck up and "bit" us. I'll bet if you look carefully, you'll find others, too. Put your people in search of them, and when they find one, reward them.

## CHAPTER 2

# GOLD NUGGETS
# BECOME A PROSPECTOR

Picture an old prospector with his donkey during the California gold rush days. He constantly had to keep his eyes peeled for gold nuggets strewn among the hills. Strewn throughout these pages are "nuggets" that can be more valuable to you than gold; if you recognize them, and pick them up.

Invite the Good Lord to walk with you on your journey through this book. He has promised to go with you every step of the way(if you invite Him), even through the valley of the shadow of death. Good prospecting, my friend.

### Does Your Funeral Home "Stand Out"?

When people drive by your funeral home, do they look twice? Is it illuminated? Is your sign really attractive, and is the lettering large enough so people can easily read it from their cars? Is the sign illuminated at night? For that matter, if electricity costs won't allow you to illuminate your entire building, at least have your sign well lit. I still remember a small bank in Cincinnati(where I studied embalming). There was a small decorative water fountain on their rather small front yard, but it shot a spray of water probably twenty feet or so into the air. It was illuminated, with the colors alternating, and it changed the atmosphere of the entire building. If you did that near your illuminated sign, erected a flag pole with both Old Glory and your state flag, and planted some nice shrubbery and flowers everyone would pause and notice.

A landscape professional may be one of the best investments you could ever make. Take a ride around your town, or the next community you find yourself in. What are some of the places that stand out to you? If you want people to consider you the best let your facilities radiate the excellence. I don't have to mention that your hedges should be trimmed, the lawn mowed, and cigarette butts cleaned up. You'll feel good about yourself, and everybody will feel good about you too. Is your parking lot well illuminated? The power company where our funeral home was located offered free lighting consultation, and for just a few dollars a month, illuminated the entire building from a light pole across the street. Are your awnings tattered? Consider indoor/outdoor carpet on your front steps. Is your entranceway attractive? Is the entranceway well lighted? No one wants to walk into a dimly lit building, much less a funeral home!

I need to say one thing about your rest rooms, and the overall cleanliness of your facilities. Some people (women especially, if they favor your competitor, will look for things to find fault with even little things). "Some people will kick if they're in swimming!" If you plan ahead you can tackle one major improvement project each year, and gain a public relations benefit by doing it. Your neighbors will definitely notice, and talk about the project with other neighbors. Contractors will talk among themselves, and traffic going by will notice activity around your place, and mention it to others. Be sure you mention the project in your holiday newsletter.

When a clergyperson shows up with a family to make funeral arrangements, welcome them! Take a little time to explain overhead costs, cemetery prices, FTC and OSHA regulations, salaries and taxes. Except for taxes, clergy have all the other headaches you do(and then some). They'll appreciate the fact that you hire professionals and pay them well. A large part of their lives have been spent in education, so they'll understand. I appreciate how a clergyperson feels. They come into a nicely furnished funeral home, see an expensive casket, top of the line funeral cars and a room full of beautiful flowers, and someone passes him or her an envelope with less money in it than someone paid for one of the vases. It's really an insult. When the funeral director forgets to pay him, it's easy to imagine the worst. One of the most sensible things we ever did was to have families make out their own checks to the minister, cemetery, and all the other people involved in the service(we would give those involved their checks from the family). Try at least to get a sense of what a fair honorarium would be. Our firm invited all the clergy in the area for an informal workshop and talked about their feelings on the subject. (Then there's the guy in my town that insisted the family give him 25% of whatever the funeral bill was!)

Sometimes Protestant clergypersons insisted that all caskets be closed in church during funerals. It's very frustrating, but I found several ways to deal with it: Have flowers arranged ahead of time at the church and invite family to have a visiting hour at your funeral home with the casket open before the church service, and then arrive at the church in a group. Another option is to have a viewing in an adjacent room from the main sanctuary, then close the casket and have bearers wheel it into the sanctuary just before the service. Yet another option is to open the casket in the adjacent room following the funeral. In the latter case, don't forget to notify the cemetery of delay. It's better to schedule a specific time for burial the next day, if you expect the funeral is going to drag on. Perhaps the best way is to leave the casket open until just before the services, then close it with everyone watching. A final option is to open the casket at the graveside.

## KIDS

Pay special attention to young children if parents bring them for visiting hours. Sooner than you think, these are the people who will be making decisions about who to call, what kind of service that will be ordered, and because they are so young, *they'll remember every kindness.* They're grieving and they're scared.

When it's convenient, take the parent(s) aside and explain that you have some things a child can do. Show them the Etch-a-sketch, the grief coloring book, drawing paper, crayons and washable marking pencils. Ask the child to draw something they remember doing with the deceased loved one. When it's done, ask the parent to go with you and the child so he or she can place it in the casket. A letter to the loved one by an older child(even an adult)which could be placed in the casket helps that person express some of the unsaid things that need to get out. Suggest they share the "letter" with another family member(or at the service)before placing it in the casket (or cremains). A number of older grandchildren have gotten together and written a composite letter of their fondest memories and one of them has read it at the service. There's an old saying that, "He who takes a child by the hand, takes the parent by the heart."

Suggest to parents that they bring their young children in separately to see their loved one when no one else is there, so they can ask questions, see the flowers, and allow parents to debunk any misconceptions a child might have about death. This became so popular that we extended it to keeping someone on duty between visiting hours so anyone, especially family from away, could stop in.

Check out my book <u>Honey the Rockhound</u> for grieving kids (ages 8-14) on the internet at Trafford.com. The E-book can be purchased for $3.99. There are a number of ways kids can get involved with the grieving process. Not only that, what they learn can empower them to help others as time goes on.

## Protecting The Elderly

If an elderly parent dies, and the other parent and adult children are present, the children will often act in a condescending way toward the parent, and try to shield them from anything that has to do with the removal. It's hard to be pushy with the children who will be making arrangements, however, if you know the surviving parent, try to have the children let you just speak to them, reassuring them that you are going to do everything just like you would if the deceased were your very own loved one. Reassure them that everything is under your care, and they can rest easier. Include an elderly parent in as much of the conversation as possible, even if they seem over-medicated or "out of it." (Discourage anyone from taking out-of-the-ordinary medication, as sooner or later the person has to face the reality, and it's better to do it with others around than by themselves at a later time.)

**CHAPTER 3**

# YOUR HERD OF CONTENTED COWS

The owner of a local restaurant and I were talking one day, and he said, "My dad was a dairyman. He worked for Carnation Milk. I was so proud of him," he exclaimed. "He had a *herd of 'contented' cows*." I thought to myself, "Wouldn't it be great if we could say as employers, I've got a staff of contented people on the job, as contented as those cows." If we can help someone who is carrying a load of grief get rid of it, it will go a long way toward their being "contented." Here are some "nuggets" that can help you keep a contented crew.

## Eight "Do-Mores"

Do more than exist, **live**. Do more than touch, **feel**. Do more than look, **observe**. Do more than read, **absorb**. Do more than hear, **listen**. Do more than listen, **understand**. Do more than think, **ponder**. Do more than talk, **say something**.

## Nine Essential Traits Of Success

1. Take responsibility for your actions.
2. Always focus on solutions, not problems.

3. Do the most important tasks first.
4. Have a useful goal: One that benefits others first.
5. Create a logical plan to achieve your goal.
6. Work hard to follow the plan.
7. While helping yourself, help others.
8. Learn whatever is needed to complete the plan.
9. When you're ready to quit, work one more day.

## Motives

Employers who understand the three motives that drive people are usually more successful:

**The achievement oriented person** likes to achieve clear standards of excellence and tests themselves against other people. They want concrete evidence from credible sources. They thrive on outperforming the norm. They always create breakthrough methods and products. An achievement oriented manager may not realize that others do not share his or her ambitions.

**The affiliation minded person** works best with people he or she is comfortable around, and trusts. They enter relationships for the sake of the relationship, not for gain or influence. Their number one concern is the quality **of their relationships.**

**The third type of person is motivated by influence.** Their greatest achievement is to beat the competition. They are greatly motivated when they are able to influence and motivate others around them. They delight in convincing someone of their point of view, have an influence on those in power. The question for those of us in management is: How do we help these people channel their energy in the best way?

## Praise People Immediately

When someone does a job well, tell them what they did right. Tell them how good you feel about it. Tell them how it helps the organization. Encourage him or her to do more of the same. Shake hands with them in such a way that it's clear to them that you support their success. Reward them in some way, not necessarily financially.

## To Reprimand

Always do it privately! Don't put it off. Do it ASAP. When you tell them what was wrong, be specific! Express *your feelings* about the situation, in no uncertain terms. Allow time for your feelings to sink in. Shake hands with them, so they understand that you are still on their side. Reaffirm how much you value them, but not this situation. Then let them know that the situation is over, end of story.

**Take any and all suggestions seriously!** Concentrate on what the other person is saying. Let them talk 80% of the time. Try hard to understand their point of view. Ask questions that can't be answered with a yes or a no answer. Have empathy. Turn off your own personal problems. Tune in on attitude. Think in mental pictures. *Do not interrupt.* Avoid making assumptions. Listen to what's **not** being said. *There may be a "real" reason behind what's being said, or not said.*

## Ho Hum, Just Another Graveside Service

*"Just" another graveside service for us, but to that family, it's the most important thing in their lives right now.* Here are some of the things you can do to make that service memorable, and not just ho hum for that family.

- A nice looking table or stand for the urn. An appropriate (velvet?) cover.
- Plenty of good-looking imitation green (for grave).
- Folding or canvas chairs for the family and elderly.
- Awnings or plenty of umbrellas.
- Battery operated P/A system. Appropriate background music.
- Guest book, and pass-outs with the deceased person's photo.
- A program with the person's obit and a photo as a pass-out is nice.)
- Acknowledgement cards for flowers.
- Flag and memorabilia displayed appropriately.
- Flowers arranged appropriately on racks
- Program if there is more than one speaker.
- Understanding of timing between speakers, and honor guard or fraternal organization.
- Planning where to move coach to allow other cars to exit cemetery following committal.
- Understanding with cemetery so family does not feel rushed.
- Little maps if people at the end of the procession might get lost from funeral home or church. Cold water for family after service on a hot day.
- If there is a vault, be sure the cover is displayed for service.

## A word about vault covers:

We must always guard our integrity. We need to do everything possible to let the family see the vault cover either before it goes on the vault, or as it is being placed on it for the last time. Sometimes the cemetery will instruct the vault company driver to leave the cover on the truck. It saves them time, and it's much easier. However if there is an opportunity for the funeral home, OR THE VAULT

COMPANY, to do a switch(or swap)this is where it could be. The family who has bought a nice vault is proud that they could do that for their loved one. As they drive up to the cemetery, and the cover is displayed, there is a great deal of pride and satisfaction when they see the massive cover sitting there. If there is trouble getting the cemetery to allow the cover to be displayed, they(the superintendent, and even the Board of Directors) need to know about it, and know why.

In a subtle way, communicate to the family that so and so from the funeral home is going to stay until the cover is placed on the vault. It may be necessary to have a family member stay with your staff at the cemetery to witness the cover being placed on the vault. Be sure the family gets the warrantee on the vault if there is one. Knowing you or your staff stayed at the cemetery is assurance to the family that everything was done as if it were for your own loved one.

There cannot be any hint of mistrust. The harsh reality is that if the family cannot see the cover, they are deprived of trust in you and their satisfaction with the vault. There is one other benefit for you, when someone stays at the cemetery until the cover is secure. Pretty soon you get on a first name basis with the Superintendent and his crew. During summer months many cemeteries hire extra help with mowing etc. These kids will go home and mention to their parents that Mr. So and So from __ funeral home was at the cemetery today. He's a nice guy, and he stays around until the cover is on the vaults. Subtle P/R?

I had a constant battle with one vault company's drivers that just couldn't get it in their head that canvas chairs at the gravesite were important to me. You may have to carry some in your trunk if they refuse to oblige you.

Always be sure the head of the person being buried is on the West side of the grave. Keep it consistent, so no one can embarrass you later.

Be sure you can be proud of the green your cemetery is using. It's better to for you provide a good looking green even if they use it for your competitor, than to be embarrassed when your family buys a nice vault and the cemetery uses a battered green. One of the larger cemeteries in our area favored a competitor of ours. They intentionally used beat-up old green when we had a burial there. They didn't seem to have any pride themselves. I don't have the answer for that one, unless it's go set up your own equipment, or have the vault company stay at the cemetery until after the cover is on your vault.

*Another Strategy on a different topic:* **Here are some things not to do while listening.**

Don't say to yourself while they're speaking, "This is what I'm going to say, to reply to the person.". Don't just hear what you want to from someone talking. Understand everything that is being said.

Don't try to second guess what the person is "really" thinking. Don't let your mind wander while the other person is talking. You may miss an important point. Be sure not to interrupt to make your points. It may shut down valuable interaction. Value whatever is being said. Don't discount it because you don't feel the person talking has the required knowledge of the subject(don't presume to judge the person's knowledge of the subject matter). By the same token, don't "buy" everything the other person says.

Don't allow yourself to become bored and stop listening. The other person may have some valuable points to communicate.

## More Strategies:

**Legal help:** Always get legal help when negotiating leases and contracts.

**Taxes:** We are sitting on shifting sands as far as taxes, especially where Federal taxes are concerned. One rule has always been: never use State or Federal tax figures when computing local taxes. Know your tax assessor. Watch out for double taxation on things like air conditioners; overvaluation; depreciation; misclassification of equipment.

**Your checkbook** should always be balanced by someone other than the person writing the checks. Number withdrawal slips in the petty cash box. Have a rule: "No borrowing money and no cashing checks."

**Phone bills:** Beware of missing times and digits on phone bills. If they are missing it's probably an error. Have written notes on all calls to be returned.

**If you are audited:** the IRS web page is www.IRS.gov. Request an "Audit Guide for Funeral Homes"(under the "Market Segment Specialization Program). It I/Ds key issues and mistakes and helps you to organize better.

**Don't consolidate loans** for debt reduction. Concentrate on the one with the highest interest. Pay that one off, and concentrate on the next one. Most of your creditors will have the same problems you do, only ten times worse.

**If someone asks** you to make a commitment, find out what difference it will make if you can't meet their date. Avoid words like *hopefully, I'll try, probably, if I can, I don't know, nobody told me.*

**Change negatives to positives. Encourage, try to help everyone feel good about themselves.**

CAUTION: Never use scented deodorizers in company cars or toilets(or in, or around the casket). Never burn scented candles. Some people are very allergic. Ask your female employees not to use highly scented perfumes, hair spray, body lotions etc. for the same reason.

**Do You have a superhero?**

**Everyone should have someone who can step into his or her shoes, and run the business in case of a serious illness or injury. Groom your replacement!**

Those making these recommendations tell us to offer that person a package they can't refuse. Offer some kind of profit sharing or partnership in a training agreement, and a legal covenant agreement not to compete. A son or daughter may want to come into the business later on, and contingency plans should be in place, but so many times I have seen children go into another profession, leaving the parent no alternative except to sell. Your superhero could well be the one to mentor your son or daughter, while you back your own nose off the grindstone a bit.

The qualifications you want to be looking for are enthusiasm, integrity, eagerness to learn, and the ability to take over. If possible promote from within your organization. By all means treat that person like royalty! Don't fear your superstar will go into competition with you. With the noncompetitive covenant, and some kind of profit sharing contract, he or she will stay, out of loyalty. Teach them everything there is to know(mentor them)about your business. The more they know the more valuable they are to you.

**Did you know that** nationally, 80% of management's time is spent unraveling yesterday's goof; that 50% of managers break down emotionally each year; that only one percent of all companies do any kind of employee training; that customers are lost each year due to discourtesy, or because someone was offended? Find out what people want and do more of it. By the same token, find out what they do not like and do less of it.

## Are You Involved In Disaster Planning?

With floods, tornados, ice storms and now terrorism, I have no doubt you are into disaster planning big time. Congratulations. Most funeral professionals are. Is your community involved with you, or is it just the professionals? Have you considered a planning event for churches, scout troops, civic and fraternal organizations?(They could become feeding centers and shelters.) How much is the business community involved? Soup kitchens and food pantries are also on the front line, and would be the first to feel a pinch if anything big happened. You could be the one to put everybody together. It's amazing how much community organizations can contribute when people are motivated and work together.

Just before Y2K I lived in a little town where different people from several organizations got together and formed a committee to plan for what could have been. We stored emergency food in several places, bought a generator to install in one of the churches, and passed out flyers to all homes giving them suggestions on how to prepare. From that little bit of effort, several county Emergency Preparedness people copied our plan. We were ready for the worst.

## The Queen's Throne

Sometimes making someone feel special pays off. I witnessed the tactic and copied it very effectively for the rest of my career. I had set up the "front room" of the funeral home for a funeral. About an hour before the family was due to arrive the boss came in, removed the chairs in the front row and replaced them with extra nice chairs(not huge overstuffed chairs, but medium-sized, comfortable sitting room type chairs.) In the middle of the row, he placed one extra nice chair. It spoke volumes about the funeral and what it represented to that family. I watched as the family arrived. The widow went directly to the extra nice chair in the middle of the front row and sat down. Her immediate family gathered around her and sat in the other nice chairs. The center chair was the place of honor. It gave her the extra status she needed.

## Up Front Where All The Action Is

I planned to ride in the lead car in every funeral procession so I could be at the grave first and keep the lead car from taking off and leaving everyone else behind. One day the guy driving the bearers' car was a little too heavy on the pedal, going through town, so I asked him to slow down a little. He ignored me. A little further on he was leaving everyone else way behind so I asked him again. "Will you shut up," he snarled. "I'm Chief of Police in ___ "(A sizeable Maine city)and I escort all the funeral processions through town!" "Yessir!" My father(a funeral director) got criticized because he took his funeral processions through town too fast. The other guy took them through too slow! He got the jump on my dad, because he was the first one to have everyone drive with their headlights on.

## We carried amulets of ammonia in case someone fainted.

Don't break one, and stick it up close under someone's nose! Begin five or six inches away. It's easier and causes less stress.

Slowly place the amulet closer and closer, and the person will come to(UNLESS you know the person is faking the faint for attention). When that happened to me, I was not careful how close I brought the ammonia to the person's nose. I found that cold water was the best thing there was for calming someone down if they were having a hard time.

## 10 Ways To Get People To Do Business With You

Be polite, patient, not crude, or gruff. Keep your word. Keep people's best interests at heart. They like those who seem to be expert. They tend to do business with people who are well groomed, people they like, who keep busy and appear to be successful. They prefer people with the same interests(golf, pets, kids, etc.). They like people who will listen and seem genuinely interested in them. They also like people who are accommodating, save them time and money, and make their lives easier.

## No more errors in the obits, WOW!

This is usually 100% fool proof. During the initial stages of making arrangements, and taking the information for the obituary, there were two of us present with the family. When it was time for the family to make a casket selection, one of us went with the family into the show room, and the other headed for the typewriter(word processor). By the time the family had returned from the show room, and completed the financial arrangements, the person typing the obituary was usually finished. We made additional copies so each family member there had a copy to read. We found that with several family members reading the "proof" they would find mistakes, and remember things that should have been included. If we were not able to complete the typing before the family left the funeral home, we made it a point to call them later and read it to one of the key players. I don't remember any complaints from families that had an opportunity to at least hear the obituary read. We found that there was another advantage to having two people with the family at first; that was to have one of us be a "go-fer" while the other carried out the interviw. For example, if a clergyperson needed to be called, one of us could go to a different room and make that call. The same thing with a hairdresser, cemetery sexton, or soloist. We were surprised at how much time it saved.

## What does your church truck say about you?

If the tires are worn and grubby, people WILL notice when you take a casket into church, or wheel it down the aisle at your funeral home. It might just be worth the small investment to get a new model.

## Rows Upon Rows

I still visit funeral homes where chairs are lined up in rows either along the walls or as if there were going to be a service when it's calling hours. It's so much more "homey" and relaxing to have little groupings of nice chairs, better than chapel chairs, but not huge over-stuffed ones. Place just a few, with a nice lamp and an end table, like you would place in your living room or den. By doing things this way, as people gather, they can comfortably talk. As more people gather, add chapel chairs to each little group, a few at a time. It requires a little more work, but it means your staff is interacting with the family and friends(One more way to makes people feel "special").

If things get busy during visiting hours, go to the widow, or, immediate family, and quietly ask them if they would like to have you bring them a cup of coffee or tea, fix it, and bring it to them with a paper towel folded under it. Always be able to get a cup of cold water. P.S. always be prepared to clean up for the person who is sick on the rug.

## Don't cover a nice casket with the flag

Fold it and place it by the deceased's shoulder. If it's a closed casket, you will probably have a family floral arrangement which needs to go on the casket anyway, and the flag can be placed beside it folded.

## "Special Attention"

Everyone craves "special attention." Tap into that desire by treating everyone who arrives at a funeral as someone special. Touch a woman (especially an older woman) on the arm, and "escort" her to her seat asking her "would you like to sit here?" As older people leave their seats following a service, stand close to the end of the row and touch the elbow or arm of every older person that steps out into the aisle. They will especially appreciate the courtesy; and another thing, many older people are a little "wobbly" on their feet when they first get up from being in one position for a long period of time.

It is important that sometime, while the family is at the funeral home or church for funeral or memorial services, that everyone there has an opportunity to greet the family. Never underestimate the value of the hug, the handshake, or the personal contact someone from away gives the grieving family. Even if time is limited, give people that opportunity to express their condolences. They may not get to the cemetery or a reception following the services.

Try to have a photo of the deceased person on the program (hand-out). Many people still like to have a keepsake they can put away and take out to look at once in awhile.

## Cutthroat Competition

How much of your business are you willing to hand over to Old Cutthroat and his buddy Bait N. Switch, before you "grab the bull by the horns"? Put your mind in neutral for a minute, and consider this: I'll bet a nickel that within the last week or so someone you know well bought _something_ that was advertised as a "special. "At Thanksgiving, especially, we all march down to the super market and buy a turkey that's sold well below cost, because it's advertised as a "special." Does anyone think about the ethics of it? Not for a minute! Does it bother anyone that the price of the turkey is being "subsidized" by something else? Heck, no! Neither does anyone bat an eye when they know they're paying extra for those fancy goodies we all "want" and sure as the dickens don't need. **We buy what we want to buy, pay extra for _them_ and don't even give it a second thought.**

Most of us today are used to looking for "good deals" and we buy impulsively without thinking everything through. So when the funeral home sleazebags advertise a fantastic price, many people forget loyalties, or integrity, and jump at the price. The sad thing is, many people today are _forced_ by economic pressures to seek out the lowest prices on **_everything_**.

Because you're already set up for it, why can't you give them _MORE_ service for the same money? Instead, most of us go out and spend the big bucks for advertising programs and overlook a wonderful P/R opportunity that's right there under our noses, that doesn't cost a dime!(I never could figure out where it cost us any more to provide the _best_, than it did to be sloppy.)Why can't you do what they do along with top quality service?

**When the direct disposal guys** advertise their "deal," they know very well the urn, extra services, marker, keepsake locket, sundry items etc. are going to make up the difference(**at your expense**)between their price on the direct disposal and a handsome profit.

Please Explain To Me Why <u>You</u> Can't Do The Same Thing? Many very successful firms still get the big bucks for cremations. However, the cremation outfits, like mean dogs, are nipping at their heels, taking a bite here and a bite there, making life miserable, while skimming off the cream(profit).

## Why Take *Only One* Piece Of The Pie When You Can Have The Whole Darned Thing?

ADVERTISE THIS WAY

"We'll Meet Old Cutthroat's Prices
And Give You Much Better Service.
We Do Everything For Your Family,
As We Would For Our Very Own.
A B C Funeral Home"

Every time the public sees the name of the disposal outfit in the obituaries it registers. Sure it's subconscious, but it's the other guy's name that registers! You pay big bucks for advertising just so people can have your name subconsciously register in their minds. Consider using that advertising buck to offer a better price to your families. There's a *lot* of free P/R that could be yours. Figure that into the equation.

You don't sell markers or stones? Why not? You can subcontract to have a cement foundation laid for a bronze marker or stone. The trade journals are full of advertisers just begging you to take 'em on.

One argument I've heard over and over again is, "It's unethical to charge a family that's having a full funeral more for professional services than I charge for a family that chooses cremation." It's unethical for a store to charge more for turkey in July than it does in November? I just don't see the difference. Some people don't care if the walnuts, cranberry sauce and stuffing mix do cost a little more to subsidize the turkey. They're going to go where *they think* the turkey is the cheapest! People don't care! They know darned well the turkey is being subsidized and they're going to buy it there anyway. People who are looking for a "deal" on cremation(or a funeral)don't care a whit **about _anything else_ but themselves**. These are tough times. We have to make the tough decisions! People would Rather Do Business With _You_. How Many Of Them Call You First for a price? They're "Programmed To Look For The Best Deal." Give It To 'em!

## You Also Represent Integrity And Quality

*PEOPLE STILL LIKE GOOD SERVICE AND INTEGRITY. IT MEANS A LOT MORE THAN YOU REALIZE. OFFER THEM BOTH. THE DIRECT DISPOSAL GUYS OPERATE ON VOLUME. WITHIN A VERY SHORT TIME YOU COULD HAVE THAT VOLUME FOR YOURSELF.*

Put in a line of Bronze Markers, Monuments, Keepsake Urns, Memorial "stuff", Books, Tapes, Videos, etc. Seriously consider the Grief Recovery Resource Center(explained in detail in the funeral director section of the Crash Course In Grief Recovery in the last part of this book). And If You Still Haven't Gotten Around To it, Start Your Own Grief Recovery Program—Get With It! I go into detail with that concept in the funeral home section of the grief recovery book.

**The Grief Recovery Resource Center Could Very Well Be The WAVE OF THE FUTURE!**

## Why Not Have A Special "Deal" For Price Shoppers That Want A Traditional Funeral?

You know the difference between the 18 gauge steel, seam welded casket and the 22 gauge tin can. Sadly the public doesn't. Be sure the price shopper knows what he's getting, for example, special fancy handles and a pretty lining. The point I'm making is, have a special low quality, good-looking casket for the person who want's a "deal". I think price shoppers should know what makes a deal a deal. **EDUCATE THEM. Once they know what makes a deal a deal, and they know you can offer them as good a deal(or better)as the other guy, they will talk seriously with you.** Remember, many price shoppers are price shopping because of serious financial hardship. They will really appreciate what you do for them. Not only that, they'll tell all of their family and friends about what a good deal you gave them! I know, it's worked great for me.

When talking with a price shopper, ask what items the direct disposal, or cremation guy's price includes? (For example, the cremation container—a cardboard box or wooden?) Does their price include writing the obituary and the newspapers' billing? Temporary storage of remains prior to cremation and the cost of the crematory itself? Does it include prayers at the cemetery and family's presence at the burial? Does it include embalming and viewing? Be emphatic about what *your price does and does not include*? Right here let me say, if they choose your firm, and the body is embalmed, be ready for a viewing, whether or not they contracted for it ahead of time. Someone from away may have strong feelings about it! If the casket is opened, be sure the body is presentable with cosmetics, stockings, hands positioned and hair washed. *P.S. Keep in mind the anger factor for everyone experiencing grief.*

Be sure to communicate that newspapers do charge for placing an obituary and listing calling hours and services. Have a clear understanding about payment to the newspapers. It may be wise to have a list of questions to ask callers who are inquiring about pricing. The family who calls(or comes in) for a price quote needs to know that when they finish talking to you, *they're getting a much better deal from you than they ever could from your competitor!*

Make them feel very special! It's better to have that family at your funeral home, and give them extra attention and service, than read about them at the competitor.

**THERE IS ONE THING I FIND DETESTABLE. IT IS THE FUNERAL HOME THAT ALSO RUNS A DISCOUNT OPERATION. IF A FAMILY CALLS ONE TELEPHONE NUMBER THEY PAY ONE PRICE. IF THEY CALL ANOTHER NUMBER THEY PAY ANOTHER PRICE. IS THAT DECEPTION? IS IT STEALING WHEN THEY TAKE MORE MONEY FROM ONE PERSON THAN FROM ANOTHER FOR THE SAME SERVICE?**

## Clothing

Keep an inventory of inexpensive white shirts for men, underwear for men and women, and things like inexpensive nylons and bras for women, and used neckties for men. The cost of providing those essentials is very low. In conversation, it's a good feeling to be able to say, "she has stockings on." Also, occasionally it's necessary to open the foot panel of the casket. Sometimes a family would bring in a man's tattered shirt. We replaced it. We often cut pieces of a lace shawl to place in the neckline of a low cut dress. We bought suits, nice dresses and sports coats from the Salvation Army, Red

Cross, and other thrift stores for welfare situations, rather than F.H. suppliers. The quality was always better.

**A passing thought:** We always planned to leave a family alone in our casket showroom after we had explained about the different kinds of caskets. Unless a family made a decision right away and came out to tell us, we took the dress, if it was a lady, or the suit coat or sports jacket, if it was a man, and laid it in the casket for the family to see. If there was a question between two caskets, we showed the garment to them in each one. It seemed that the longer the family took browsing, the better quality they selected, and generally, the more satisfied the family seemed to be.

## TIPS FOR A GREAT PUBLICITY RELEASE.

Take full advantage of everything your company or your employees do that is newsworthy. Has someone on your staff been appointed to a board of directors of an organization like the Red Cross, become a coach of a sports team, reached a milestone in community service, or received an award or a license related to funeral service? So many times personal achievements are not communicated to the newspapers and could provide valuable public relations for your firm. The following information will help you submit a powerful press release. If you're fortunate enough to have a community television station, submit that information to them also.

1. Get to know the local newspaper reporter if there is one and feed the information to him or her.
2. Use as many names as possible. Supply them with as many photos as you can.
3. Invite the reporter to a working lunch.
4. Date your article. If possible hand deliver it, and ask for suggestions and help.
5. Identify yourself and how to contact you.

6. Use large enough font for easy reading.
7. Find out the day the papers go to press. Feed competitive papers the information so both get the same information at the same time. For example if you have a daily paper, and a weekly paper, make sure the release is fresh and new to both so the daily paper releases the information on the same day the weekly releases the same story. Your weeklies usually go into more detail, and print more names.
8. At the end of each publicity release, do a brief summary of the project.
9. Don't favor one news source over another. One of them will surprise you someday with a feature story and photos,

## Do you have a prep room check off sheet?

It would tend to assure that everyone took the required time and did not pull any sloppy workmanship. It would also be a double check on things such as fingernails, eyebrow trim, nostril disinfection, and cotton support while embalming.

A flow chart for every deceased person coming through your facility should be a gentle reminder that things were accomplished in a timely manner. An initial after the task would help anyone following up on details, such as ordering the vault, confirming bearers, seating, etc.

## Misunderstanding And Communications

These are the two biggest problems in funeral service today. Be aware of them. The biggest problem of all is that staff is not aware of what management is thinking, or doing. For that "herd of cows" to be "contented" there has to be communication. Daily planning is necessary, so everyone is on the same frequency. It's also wise sometime after a funeral, to go over all the details. "How could we have done it better?" "Were there unexpected problems that we could have handled better?" Another area where problems occur is between employees making a home removal during the night, and getting messages communicated correctly with the ones taking over in the morning. Be sure to get a phone number for a follow-up call to the family. For example, you might say, "Did I understand(night time employee's name) to say, you planned to be here at 11.00 AM and that you would bring Mr. Smith's veterans' papers with you? Did you remember his dentures, and a picture for the paper? Do you need a ride?"

You might want to consider a small card with check off items to leave with the family as a reminder in the morning. (Clothing, dentures, photo for paper, VA and SS information, lot number for cemetery, etc.)

There was an area of miscommunication that I often found frustrating. That was when someone who was not going to work the funeral had visiting hours the night before, and forgot to communicate last minute changes in seating, line-up of family cars, or last minute instructions regarding flowers, etc. A note or check-off-list would be handy. Ninety-nine percent of all problems on the job could easily be ironed out by adopting the small support group principle spelled out in the "Crash Course In Grief Recovery" section later on in the book. The staff support group meets periodically(usually weekly)and talks about everything and anything pertaining to the job, problems on the job, or at home, anything. When a serious problem arises, there is usually grief associated with it in some form or another, and the facilitator, understanding grief issues, along with input from others in the group, can help the person work through their issues.

Sooner or later everyone has problems, and knowing others in the group can, and are willing to help, is a great shot in the arm! Consider it seriously. It will do more to improve "contentment" within your "herd" than you can imagine.

## Don't Be Fooled by The Bloody Blade

Did you ever think you would like to have a branch chapel on the other side of the city, or in a neighboring town? Here are some tips on expanding, or making more money with the one you already have.

When Eskimos are having a problem with wolves, and I presume polar bears, they use an interesting strategy. They soak a long knife blade with blood, and freeze it. This is repeated several times until there is a thick coating of blood on the blade. Then they imbed the handle of the knife in the ice, freezing it solid. The wolf comes along and smells the blood, At once the wolf begins to lick the blade. The blade is razor sharp, and it doesn't take long before the wolf has cut it's tongue. Tasting the warm blood, it licks faster and faster, eventually cutting it's tongue enough so it bleeds to death. That is similar to a funeral director sensing that the location for a new chapel is enticing.(He smells the blood. He can almost taste it.) Then he becomes eager, and licks the blade. He sets up a chapel without thinking through on the long range strategy, and sets himself up to bleed badly financially. Sometimes they even bleed to death.

**Here are a few things to consider before opening your branch chapel:**

Someone needs to be there, at least during business hours, so if people drop by to check the place out, there is someone to talk with. To me if there is not enough potential to support a funeral director, there should not be a branch at that location. If there is no one there full time, at least have a retired couple living on the premises. (Preferably, someone from the neighborhood, or the surrounding area.) No one wants to have their loved one left alone in a dank, dimly lit branch chapel, especially if they are not sure of the security around the place. There needs to be a considerable amount of ongoing activity at the place. Lawn mowed, cars and funeral coaches coming and going most of the time, and lights on during the evening. You can create a considerable amount of activity by bringing the hearse over to the chapel and have someone polish it, or just move the cars around in the driveway so it looks busy. Don't think that just because it's smaller than your main facility, that it should be second rate. Have an open house with a "dedication" by area clergy. Serve refreshments. Print a brochure about "our business history."

Whoever is there representing the owner, should be at least somewhat active in the community. The same things apply with the branch chapel as with the main office. Read the section on advertising, and public relations. The public is not going to break tradition, step out of the routine, or try someone, or someplace new, unless they know the new manager, or have a good excuse to do it. They want someone that's going to be part of their community. Someone they can identify with, recognize when they see them in a local store, or coffee shop, or school activity.

People are not going to be "different," or try someone new, without a good reason. They want to know they are going to receive service when they go there, otherwise you will be licking the bloody blade, and hemorrhaging badly with your new investment. We had a branch in a nearby town, with a resident living at the facility. Our reputation was well established, yet the public drove almost twenty miles away and did business with someone they knew, before they would call us. It was not until I (one of the business partners) actually moved to that town, and became active in the community, that people trusted us enough to care for their loved ones. The residents did not mind that much of my time was spent at our main facility, but they expected me at the branch facility, most of the time when there was a family there. We hired a local person who was retired to do most of the visiting hours and help us with the actual funerals, but the bare facility was very much like the bloody blade. There, yes, and bleeding us to death until we realized we needed to be there to make it successful!

Don't forget the illumination of the building, flag, and nice sign. Be sure the sign is big enough to read from the road, and illuminate it all night(seriously consider illuminating a small colored fountain.) Give the locals something to talk about: make it look like you intend to stay! Don't forget the news release and publicity release to the local paper. Be sure you understand the grief recovery program, and explain it briefly at your open house. Send out a holiday letter to the area. Be sure to offer to do grief recovery workshops for churches, nursing homes and hairdressers in the new area. I wish you the very best!

**I know what I'm talking about. I've seen it happen a number of times over the years. In one instance, I literally saw an owner "bleed to death" (financially) because he *refused* to follow my advice regarding these principles. He had three branch facilities, and he lost them all. How sad.**

## False Economy

Here's a tidbit of information that will save you a lot of money in the long run. Buy THE BEST of whatever it is you are buying. It will last TWICE As long, give you better service, little or no repair and you will be more satisfied because you have the best. Not only that, others who understand quality, will hold you in higher esteem. Depending on what it is, there may even be some resale value in it.

## Scrap booking

I go into this quite a bit in the Crash Course In Grief Recovery section at the end of the book. Scrapbook decorating is a growing hobby that you could easily incorporate into your recovery program. It's especially appropriate for the social support group(which I talk about later in the book)where there is much hidden talent for this type of project.

The idea is to have each family make a memorial page in your scrapbook for and about their loved one who has died. There are many ways you could do this, but the ultimate goal is to create a memorial archives for everyone your firm buries over the years, It would be a great way to improve public relations and offer future generations a place to come to read a little more about their loved one, one or more generations ago.

Eventually your widowed persons social support group might want to extend this project to include a page in the scrapbook for everyone in the area that passes on, until you are able to organize and get the social support group rolling. Start the project yourself, and be sure the scrapbook(s) are where the public can view them. Anyone with some simple artistic ability can decorate a scrapbook, and each family, doing the memorial page for their loved one, may have some unique creative ability they want to interject into the project. Be sure this is featured in your next holiday newsletter.

**Don't Overlook The Section "The Grief Recovery Resource Center" in the Crash Course In Grief Recovery**

Section later in the book. It could be a great way to offer long term grief recovery for your entire area, and certainly get your project talked about throughout the community.

## CHAPTER 4

# LET UNCLE SAM CARRY THE LOAD FOR YOU

Your business is built on one personal relationship at a time. The best way to build those relationships is personal contact. Direct mail is the second most effective way there is to solidify those relationships. The difference they will make in your public relations, is comparable to using electric lighting instead of a kerosene lantern. Direct mail is as old as the hills, but as fresh as a daisy.

**Below is a sample follow-up letter to be sent a week or so after services. This one is written primarily to a widow.\* The wording of course would be adjusted for other close family members of the deceased. Grief recovery support groups can be organized for anyone who is grieving for any reason. See the last section of this book(A Crash Course In Grief Recovery, for how-to details.)**

Be sure to send the widow a personal note at the first anniversary of the death. This will be a very important date to most widows. You will receive much more sincere appreciation from these two strategies from most widows than from anything else you could do. Also be sure you or the key funeral director that handled the services calls the widow several times following the death of her husband.

Then try to convince her to get involved with the widows grief recovery program, as explained in chapter six, and in the funeral director section in "A Crash Course In Grief Recovery." (P.S. A widowers support group is included in that section also.)

* Dear ____,

I sincerely appreciate the confidence and trust you have placed in all of us at __Funeral Home at the time of John's death. We have done everything we know to serve your family as we would our very own, during this most difficult time of your lives. I want to assure you that everything will be *strictly confidential*. Are any of your family members having a particularly hard time coping with John's death or the loss of anyone else from the past? We can probably help you, or them. Don't hesitate to call. Does someone have anything they want to talk with me about?

May I ask a very special favor of you? Would you take a few minutes and share your thoughts with me about the events surrounding John's funeral and our services? Thank you. We can't improve our services if we don't know where to begin. I've enclosed a form with some questions. Please give me your honest opinion and return the form to me in the enclosed envelope. If someone else in your family wants to comment too, ask them to do so on a separate piece of paper. They(or you)do not even have to sign the form. If someone in your family wants to just sit down for awhile and talk about the service or anything else. please have them call me. I appreciate your doing this for me more than you know.

Perhaps you've already heard that Funeral Home has several groups of recently widowed persons that get together each week for support and fellowship. They find it helpful knowing others who have also experienced the death of a loved one. I'll be contacting you within the next few weeks to see when you think you might be ready to sit down with a couple widows from our support group just to chat. Later, when you are ready, you will be welcome to join one of our support groups. I'm sure you'll be an encouragement to many others. In the meantime, call me if there's any way we can help you, or if you just want someone to talk with.

Sincerely, **To be signed by the professional who actually directed the funeral, made the arrangements and did the most to assist the family personally. It's best to have all correspondence signed by that individual.**

Another important suggestion: About three days after the services ask the director, who played the key role in making the arrangements and directing the funeral, to call the widow(or other significant family member)to touch base and see if things are going OK. Ask if there are things your firm could do to help. Is there anything they don't really understand? Do they need additional certified copies of the death certificates, etc. You will find suggestions for a family survey in the funeral director section of the "Crash Course In Grief Recovery" in the last part of this book.

## Holiday Newsletter

I need to place a disclaimer here. Our little firm never sent a holiday newsletter; however, my recycle bin is filled with newsletter and flyers that come here at all times of the year. They are very effective. We welcome some that are focused on specific topics. Having a list of activities going on in your area during the holidays is something people would place on their refrigerator. Leave a couple of blank lines for people to add items that are announced the last minute. People usually enjoy musicals, church programs, etc. especially around Christmas.

I've mentioned several projects, in the pages ahead, that could be successful, if someone wanted to tackle them. If you have any questions get back to me. For now I suggest you place them on the back burner and let them simmer while you tackle the big guns and the secret weapon.

Most people still like to read snail mail. If it's fancy, colored, and looks like an ad, it'll likely go straight into the round file. Placed in an envelope with their name and address neatly typed or handwritten and stamped with a regular postage stamp, nearly everyone will open and read it. Direct mail is still the most effective way of getting your message out there. You need to get started early, because it needs to be in people's mailbox just before Thanksgiving. Churches etc. that are planning Christmas pageants, etc, have begun work on them in the Fall. An hour or so on the phone, asking each church secretary what they have planned, *and if they know of any other activities in the area*, too, should get most of them. There's another subtle P/R boost here too. When you talk with the church(or other)secretary, you are planting a goodwill seed for your firm. *Don't forget "Y's", Boys & Girls clubs, sports and civic clubs, merchants' groups, towns or cities who sponsor events, swimming pools, and, if you are fortunate to have a college, they might be having early events, too. Don't overlook fraternal orders, veterans groups, the area orchestra, musical groups and malls. In my opinion, there are certain things a holiday newsletter should and should not do. It should briefly mention new policies and services you provide. It should offer hope for grieving people. Its should not promote prepaid burials.

Your holiday newsletter should encourage people who are grieving to get out in the community and avoid isolating. Being lonely around the holidays, especially if you've just experienced the death of a loved one is horrible! The more ways you can suggest that someone get out and get involved, the better off they'll be. They'll also appreciate you for suggesting it. That's why the memorial candlelight or Christmas Tree decoration activity is so very helpful. If your schools or community provide any kind of holiday activities *get behind them.* Offer free transportation. Communicate this in your newsletter with any community group to get them involved. Include your phone # for transportation. No, you're not running a free taxi service, but for special occasions it's great P/R. Many people with no family close by, are looking for somewhere to go just to be with people during the holidays. Be sensitive to it!

* We talked about getting *your* people involved in public relations activities. If they've done newsworthy things during the past year be sure to mention it in your newsletter.

*Computer photos work in great. The more the better. * Mail to *any* and *every* family you've served in the past. * Mail to each business and professional service in your area. * Mail to your police and fire departments. * Mail to each clergyperson in your area. * Mail to each organization, service club, charity, fraternal, social and veterans organizations, and local companies(enclose a handwritten note inviting each group to have a memorial type service for their recently deceased members).

Also in your newsletter, stress what's available in the way of support groups, activities and things to get everyone who's grieving involved in support groups. Anything to keep them from isolating. Employers will communicate these things to their employees by posting them on their bulletin boards and sharing them with their own families. Offer to conduct company memorial services free during the holidays. If you're going to offer a twenty-four hour hot line for grieving people during the holiday season, you're, of course, going to say so. You're going to invite people to stop in at your funeral home grief recovery center(it's explained in detail in the "A Crash Course In Grief Recovery" section of this book). You're going to invite them to drop in at your lounge and have a cup of hot chocolate or eggnog and chat. Invite them to bring a photo of their cherished pet that has died, and offer a book, **Honey The Rock Hound**, to anyone that does. And finally, you're going to mention that your team has recommitted to serve every family you do business with exactly as they would their own loved ones.

(I do *not* recommend sending a holiday newsletter the first holiday following a death.) The one year follow-up will be sufficient. Be careful not to double mail. (One more reason for the same professional to handle/sign all follow-up correspondence.)

## Examples for a Holiday Newsletter:

Beginning Thanksgiving day and continuing through Sunday January __ our Sally Jones and John Sullivan will be heading up a 24 hour talk line. It's for anyone who just wants to pick up the phone and talk to someone. It could be for anyone trying to cope with the loss of a loved one, but it doesn't have to be. Tell your friends about this. It's free.

Friday, Saturday and Sunday evenings we will sponsor an open door social support group through the holiday season. November 5th through January 15th there will be a holiday open house support group for any widowed person. Just drop in to our grief recovery resource center from 4:00 PM 'til 9:00 PM and visit with us.

> On December 9th there will be a special Memorial Tree Decorating Service at our chapel at 123 Broadway. It's for anyone with a loved one who has died within the past two years. It doesn't matter if the loved one has died locally, or away. Anyone is welcome. It will be led by our Gregg Moore. Everyone will be invited to place an ornament on our Memorial Tree and say a few words about the one who has died, read a poem, or tell some special thing they'd like others to remember about their loved one.
>
> Call Gregg at 456-7890 to let him know you're coming and what family members will be with you. We will have to limit one ornament for each family.
>
> Each ornament will be identified with a numbered ribbon attached to the hanger. They will be saved and either returned or held for family members after Jan.__th. There will be refreshments following the service, and if you like, we'll provide transportation for you. Just let Gregg know.
>
> Christmas Carols will be sung to the accompaniment of Jason Porter.

## Notice: To All Widowed Persons

On Friday, Dec 8th the Snowshoe Area Widowed Persons Support Group will sponsor an afternoon of fellowship for all widowed persons in the area. The event will be held from 1:00 PM to 4:00PM at the Snowshoe Community Center. Refreshments will be served. Any widowed person is welcome. They do not have to be a resident of Snowshoe. Please contact Gladys Carter at (113) 456-7890 and let us know if you'll be there and/or want a ride. The Snowshoe Council of Churches will provide Sacred Music.

**Thomas Anonymous**

## A New Course of Direction

After much prayer and deliberation, ___ Funeral Home has decided to meet our competition's discount prices on cremations and minimum service burials. We have always paid our employees more than average to assure we retained the highest qualified funeral service professionals anywhere. We have always done our part in supporting community charities and youth activities in Snowshoe. We continue to do this and at the same time offer our families *more* service, *better* merchandise and first class facilities. As always, we pledge to do *everything* for each family we serve as we would for our very own loved ones.

## New Pet Loss Service

Anyone experiencing the death of a house pet(dog, cat, birds etc.)is invited to take advantage of our new Pet Removal and Cremation Service. For a small fee we will remove the deceased pet's body from your premises for cremation. Small bronze markers and memorabilia are available at our resource center.

If you wish, markers may be displayed at our new Best Friend Memorial Park & Exercise Trail located at 1776 Horseshoe Road off Rt. 196 in Snowshoe. For a modest fee we will also facilitate a time of sharing and memory for your pet at the park, your home, or at our grief recovery center. We will also help you create laminated memorial cards with pet photos if you'd like.

*(I suggest you only charge a token fee.)*

**Funeral Directors:**

*There are tremendous P/R opportunities here, as many of us have cherished pets.*

## The Pet Lovers Exercise Trail

In case you missed the publicity in early September, __ Funeral Home has opened a pet lover's exercise trail at 1776 Horseshoe Road off Route 196. At the present time there are two easy walking trails. One is .8 mile and the other 1.3 miles. All we ask is that you utilize the plastic waste containers that are free at the gate. There is also a separate 5.3 mile riding trail for horses.(There is ample parking for horse trailers.)Call our office for info.

## Pet Lovers Support Group

On October 7th, at 6:00 PM, Armand Turcotte of ___ Funeral Home will host a Pet Lovers Support Group at our Family Resource Center for pet owners, friends and family whose pets have died this past year. Those participating will have an opportunity to share photos of and experiences with their pets. Photos of one's pets may be placed on the Pet Memorial bulletin board at the center. Please call Armand at 456-7890 for more information. Everyone who has experienced the loss of a pet this past year is welcome. Please share this information with friends and neighbors. Transportation is available by calling Armand.

Also in your newsletter, you might want to consider an artical such as the one below:

## A Bright Spot

All of us at __ Funeral Home have enjoyed our Good News Bulletin Board at the Family Resource Center. We post pictures and news articles of people and events that have been recognized for making Snowshoe a better community. We would welcome any articles you might want to contribute. Stop in and see it and check out our grief recovery resources while you're at it.*(If you are going to serve coffee, eggnog or any snacks be sure you have the proper vendor's license to do it.)* My suggestion would be to buy pastries locally and provide coffee etc.

## A Serious Moment

*Photo op*

For the past three years, Bob Gray, one of our senior staff professionals has been working with the Snowshoe Disaster Preparedness Committee. They have produced an excellent personal preparedness booklet. They are available free at our Family Resource Center. There are many helpful suggestions on getting your family ready for any kind of emergency including a power outage. Bob has offered to do disaster preparedness workshops. Give him a call if you're interested.

## Hat's off to the Men's Support Group!

*Photo Op*

This past Fall our Marvin Lowe and Dale Jones initiated a crafts project that includes wood carving, woodworking and model airplane building. Flying lessons for model airplanes are at 1:00 PM Saturday afternoons at the high school parking lot. The group is open to any widowed man. Model "loaners" are available at no cost.

## The Good Neighbor Club

Under the leadership of our Jeff Rockingham the Widower's Support group has recently initiated a project of doing odd jobs for the elderly, shut-ins, and disabled. There is no charge for their services. If you know anyone in need of help let Jeff know. The group also does errands and visits shut-ins to fellowship or play cards. They meet for breakfast each Tuesday at 7:00 AM at our Family Resource Center. If you know any man who is widowed, they would be welcomed(*Another photo op*).

## Another Exciting Project

The Good Neighbor Club has started working with the Hospice group to provide companionship for children who are grieving, or who have seriously ill parents. This group meets at ___church Saturday afternoons at 2:00 PM. There are a host of activities such as hiking, gardening, ping pong, shuffle board, drama and crafts. Contact Jeff if you know of any child who might like to be part of this group. The widowers work with kids of all ages.

## Not To Be Outdone

The ladies support group has been active this past year as well. They're contacting recently widowed persons to offer companionship and assistance with housework and shopping. In addition to their holiday support hot line they've initiated a support network calling elderly and shut-ins.

## Beckett Appointed To Red Cross Board

*Photo op*

Horace Beckett of __Funeral Home has recently been invited to become a member of the Tri-County Board of Directors for the American Red Cross. He has been an Instructor \Trainer in CPR and Advanced First Aid for several years.

## Nash Promoted to Head Coach

*Photo op*

Carl Nash Senior Embalmer at __ Funeral Home was promoted to Head Coach for the Bulldog Team in the Pop Warner Football League. The announcement was made at the annual awards banquet Nov 3rd at the Snowshoe Civic Center. Carl has been active with the league for ten years, where he played Center as a boy. This year Carl's son Bryce is playing Quarterback for the Bulldogs.

## Funeral Home Personnel To Man Salvation Army Kettles at Snowshoe Mall Again This Year

Staff and family of __ Funeral Home will again man the Salvation Army Kettles at the Mall this Christmas season. The Salvation Army is always there whenever disaster or tragedy strikes. This year the need is greater than ever according to Captain Mark Smith of the Snowshoe Salvation Army. Remember, do <u>your</u> part.

Memorial Service For <u>*Your*</u> Group This Year?

Our staff would welcome an opportunity to work with your church, business or organization during this holiday season to plan and conduct a memorial service for members who have died this past year. Our receptionist Gladys Jones is the one to talk with at our office. Let her know if there is someone from our staff you would particularly like to work with.

**CHAPTER 5**

# YOUR BIG GUNS BATTLE-TESTED AND READY FOR ACTION

The Atomic Bomb ended WW II. It was horrible beyond description, but it shortened the war by many months, probably years. However, it was not the Atomic Bomb alone that won the war. It took air power to deliver the bomb. It took many soldiers, sailors and marines who fought valiantly in the jungles of the South Pacific and the beaches in Normandy; a first class military and thousands of dedicated men and women, to actually win the war. In the Bible drama of David and Goliath, it took more than David's sling shot to bring the giant down. There were many other factors at work, or the slingshot would not have been successful.

Your secret weapon, delivered in love, is exceedingly powerful, but it, alone, will not break the competition's power or resolve. It will give you the competitive edge, and help you keep it for a long time. Used the way it's intended it will positively affect every family in your area. It will help many who are struggling to get that awful load of grief off their backs! In regard to the next weapon, see the next chapter.

These "Big Guns" are what gave our little firm in a bedroom community, doing fifty some odd calls a year, in a life or death battle with seven top flight funeral homes and a branch chapel, enough of a competitive advantage, so that when I retired, we were doing over two-hundred calls a year. It will be a long haul, as it was for us, but your firm can grow that much, and a lot more, because we hadn't <u>perfected</u> the secret weapon or these big gun strategies at that time! We had the widowed person's social support group going, but we had no idea at the time that it would be such a powerful P/R tool.

I don't think any one of these next winning strategies are more important than any of the others. They all work together and compliment one another. Here they are, not necessarily in order of effectiveness or importance.

## As Your Own

Do everything as though you were doing it for your own family members.

"Our Family Will <u>*Never*</u> Call Your Outfit Again!" It was one of those bodies that would not have fit well in any oversized casket, and we <u>*didn't*</u> *take the extra time beforehand that we should have (shoulda, woulda, coulda, the five minute rule, and the FUSS principle. We forgot all of them.) Once again Murphy's law worked perfectly.* The funeral director <u>thought</u> everyone had gone out, so he walked over to the body in the casket and literally <u>POUNCED</u> on the person's shoulders to drive them down in the casket. You guessed it! Someone WAS watching from the doorway! And, yes, you got the rest of the story right also. Keep this ritual very solemn! The deceased was probably a close friend of many of the bearers. Your attitude will be infectious as you do this! You are on center stage in the drama of life. Play your part perfectly. People want the ritual and ceremony. Give It To Them! Most of

### 101 Battle Tested P/R Strategies for Successful Funeral Directors

them will remember your attitude for the rest of their lives. It could well make the difference between them calling you or a competitor when their loved one dies!

If there are things to remove before the casket is closed for the last time, take a piece of masking tape. Fold the ends in so it will remove easily, and stick it on the lid of the casket. It will not leave a mark on the lid, but you won't forget and leave expensive jewelry on the deceased. Let me remind you, that as jewelry becomes more valuable place extra caution on removing and returning it.

Let me suggest a new rule. If you are not already doing it, have witnesses every time you close a casket for the last time! Have the bearers stand there while you close the lid on the casket. Remember the story of the funeral director who was removing jewelry as instructed. On the way back from the restroom one old couple was watching from the doorway, "See ma," the man said, "I told you them undertakers stole the jewelry off all the bodies when they closed the caskets." Have a couple of extra envelopes in your pocket to put jewelry in when you remove it.

IF IT'S NOT PARTICULARLY EXPENSIVE, PASS THE ENVELOPE TO ONE OF THE BEARERS AND ASK HIM TO GIVE IT TO THE FAMILY FOR YOU. IT SHOWS THE BEARER THAT YOU RESPECT HIM, AND GIVES HIM A LITTLE BIT OF EXTRA STATUS.

"BIG U". (PLUS THERE IS ONE MORE PERSON WHO KNOWS YOU DID REMOVE IT IN THE FIRST PLACE.) IF IT IS EXPENSIVE JEWELRY, ASK THE IMMEDIATE FAMILY AS THEY LEAVE TO WAIT IN THE NEXT ROOM WHILE YOU REMOVE IT. THEN GIVE IT TO THEM *YOURSELF* WHILE

THE BEARERS ARE STILL THERE. THEY'VE SEEN YOU TAKE IT OFF AND GIVE IT TO THE FAMILY.

Another good reason to have the bearers present is to have them watch you tenderly and gently close the cover. I had to have a vault cover removed and take a pair of transistor hearing aid glasses off a man, because I had left them on the body. I didn't realize they were hearing aids. At the time a body is placed in the casket, be sure the lid will close completely and easily. That way when it's time to close it for the last time you can take your time and put some flair into the procedure. I often placed the casket "throw" on the deceased like a shawl(not over the face).

## The removal cot.

Pay special attention to this. When we walked into a room where there was a nurse or care giver(and many times a family member)we were proud to open our cot.

Why is the appearance of your removal cot so important? Because, it reflected in a positive way our attitude and respect for the deceased person. To the grieving family, the individual who died was the most sacred thing there was to them at that particular time. Sadly that love and respect has vanished for some families, but not the majority of them!

Usually, when we went to a home or nursing home, someone was with us when we actually placed the body on our removal cot. The outer pouch was the best looking pouch we could buy. However, inside we had a pretty(light blue or green) king size pastel blanket folded up on each side from the middle. The first thing a person saw when we unzipped the outside pouch was the pastel blanket, folded up from each side, with clean, good looking straps snapped in place over the blanket. When we unbuckled the straps, and opened the blanket, anyone would see a white plastic hard stretcher, with a clean white pillow and case. Underneath the pillow, we had a clean white sheet which we placed over the deceased remains ASAP. Masks and gloves were also under the pillow.

If members of the immediate family of a person to be cremated could not be there when we made the initial removal, but were coming, and wanted to see the body, we would leave it on the cot at the funeral home until they had viewed their loved one. We opened the top of the cot so they could view their loved one's face, with the head on a clean pillow. We also brought the cot upstairs, in the funeral home, instead of having the family come downstairs to the operating room. What was seen made a subconscious lasting impression. If you already do these things, congratulations!

On another subject, a folding canvas stretcher carried in the removal car is often useful for tight places. Have straps handy. The hard plastic stretcher was great for sliding a body from a bed to the removal cot. If you cover the body first with some kind of sheet, it signifies respect and dignity. The sheet over the deceased person's nose and mouth is a line of protection against airborne bacteria or viruses. A small disinfectant spray used at that time for the nose and mouth would be appropriate.

## The five minute rule:

Take the extra five minutes and double check every detail. When my four boys were in high school, like any teenager they wanted to drive. In order to get a reduced rate on their insurance, they had to be on the honor role. The five minute rule did a pretty good job of keeping them on the honor role. What is the five minute rule? **"The difference between**

**an 'A' and a 'B' is five minutes.** In those five minutes the student can correct the mistakes that were carelessly made. By going over their work, they pick up things they forgot, correct spelling, and reinforce the lesson. Apply that rule in the funeral home and you'll be running a class "A" operation!

**F U S S: The most powerful four letter "F" word!**

Fuss five minutes more with cosmetics that don't look quite "right."

Fuss five minutes more with flowers that don't quite seem to be in harmony.

Fuss with each body as you place it in the casket. Is a dress wrinkled? Are the cuffs on a man's long sleeved shirt showing? Are the fingernails clean?

Would another five minutes fussing with an obituary honor the person better?

Fuss five minutes more with those little things that mean so much to a family.

What are we really selling? Funerals, cremations, caskets? Aren't we really selling the grieving family their day in the sun—a time to create memories, to be loved, to get the attention they crave and need at the time of a loss? The opportunity for some people at least, to feel important. Memories to cherish for the rest of their lives, and share with their family and friends.

## The "Big U" Strategy:

This is a departure from the norm, but it is very effective. It says, "pay attention to the little guy!":

It's the guy or gal who has the menial job—the garbage collector, the guy that sweeps the streets, the gal that cleans the bed pans in the nursing home. Go out of your way to make friends with these people. Seek out the person who gets left out of the conversation, the guy in the wheelchair, the unlovely, the bashful, the very old and very young. Try to make them feel like they are someone special. These people get very little recognition. You are the one giving it to them!

Strike up a conversation with them, try to get it across to them that you think that what they are doing is extremely important, and you'd like to know more about it. It's hard to do, but try to speak to everyone you meet, even if they don't want to answer. Make eye contact with everyone you speak to. Remember, a smile improves your face value. Encourage the person who is hesitant about taking the committee chairmanship you would probably like to have.

Watch for the person who's sitting on the edge of their seat, asking questions, and eager to help. Do what you can to get that person a leadership role, and be there to help them. This way you have complimented the person, and given them the opportunity to really shine. There's another thing we don't think about when we encourage(or nominate) someone else to be Chairman of a committee. You have made a good friend, and all their close friends and family will hear about it.

### Use a woman's own hairdresser whenever possible.

The difference in the way a woman who has died looks when she has her usual hair style, rather than having it done by someone who just guesses, makes all the difference in the world to those who love her.

We shampooed everyone's hair twice, once with disinfectant soap and once with regular shampoo. It was good public relations. If there was a hairdresser involved, there was no antiseptic aroma hinting of embalming chemicals. We made it known some time during the conversation with the hairdresser that we had done that. I felt sure the procedure was communicated to the woman's family, and everyone the hairdressers told about what she / he had done.

Oftentimes the hairdresser had been in contact with the woman's family before coming to our funeral home. It was almost assured. I very seldom had a hairdresser refuse to do a woman's hair. I always asked the family what they wanted to give the hairdresser, and just included that on the bill. Often a hairdresser would say there was no charge, that they wanted to do the woman's hair for the family.

Someone, half joking, once said, that a woman's hairdresser knew her better than her therapist did. Needless to say, there were strong bonds that developed between them over the years. It's at least a slight, not to invite her(or him)to do the woman's hair. Many times the hairdresser contacted the family as soon as it was convenient letting the family know how the woman looked. We almost always asked the hairdresser for suggestions regarding cosmetics. Those little suggestions made a tremendous difference in the overall appearance of the deceased woman.

The public relations value of this strategy can not be emphasized enough. If other funeral homes are not doing it, it's brand new to the hair dresser. You can be sure she or he is going to tell his or her customers and all of the other professionals in the area. Every one of his or her friends will know just how nice your professional staff really is, how clean your prep room(or dressing room) was, how nice the body looked, the extra respect you showed it, and how he or she made suggestions about the woman's cosmetics. We had a couple of hairdressers who would come in when a woman did not have her own.

## (ALWAYS wash hair and clean fingernails!)

I learned the lesson about washing everyone's hair the hard way. I had just gone to work for a gentleman, when we got a call that a middle aged woman had died. She obviously had had her hair done recently, so the boss said to be careful with the cream around her forehead, and we wouldn't have to get a hairdresser. Anyway, we placed the woman in her casket, and the family arrived. The scene is still etched in my memory. The first person to walk through the door exclaimed at the top of her voice, "They didn't even wash her hair!"

## Help everyone (men and women alike) with their coat.

Let the door go. Treat the person struggling to get their coat off and on like royalty. I saw at least four men standing in line once, following a funeral, with their coats folded over their arms, waiting for the owner of the funeral home to help them put their coats on. Giving those *people special attention, made them feel `important!* (That's when I learned what a great P/R tool that was.) P.S. Have the coat rack handy to the door.

## Organize a widows' social support group.

I had no idea how effective that group would be when I launched the original program. I wish I could hit you beside the head with a baseball bat, and say, "Pay Attention!" Do this first, if there is no group where you are. In The Crash Course In Grief Recovery, later on in the book, there's a sample letter inviting *a widow who has worked through her own grief* to help you organize a social group.

The sample letter is just one phase of the process of getting the group up and running. If you follow my guidelines, everything will eventually fall into place, even down to a detailed plan on how to put in place a political framework that will allow you to be involved, without seeming to be domineering. **Be sure all of those organizing the group have worked through their grief issues, and have had plenty of time to recover. I can't emphasize this point enough. Until a woman is ready to get out a little bit, and tackle life's issues, and wants to get out socially, she will not enjoy the group. Her heart will not be in it, and the others will not appreciate where she is coming from.** They've been there. There is an account of what happened to me when I tried to organize a social group with widows who were not ready for the social aspects of a group in "A Crash Course In Grief Recovery" at the end of this book.

It may seem like I am harping on this point. I probably am, but this whole concept was a complete surprise to me. My original intention was to get a group of widows together for some social activity, and let it go at that. The concept mushroomed into the most effective P/R program for funeral service I have ever heard tell of or seen.

## Another Important Strategy: Get involved in Community Activities(Be the Publicity Director, if Possible)

> Volunteer to be publicity director of any project. Most people are skittish about becoming a publicity director, especially if it's for a large project. Welcome the opportunity, You are an expert at taking information for obituaries. To you, it's a breeze. It places you in close contact with all kinds of people you wouldn't otherwise get to meet. Everyone will be looking to see what you wrote about them when the first publicity release comes out in the paper. There is another benefit that we don't think about when we encourage(or nominate, with his or her permission) someone else to be Chairman of the committee. You have made a friend. The person who you nominated should know that you'll be right there when the going gets tough. Don't hesitate to roll up your sleeves and get your hands dirty.

## Open Door Policy For Families

It began with us inviting a family with small children to bring their little ones in so they could see their loved one, witness the flowers, and leave a drawing in the casket. The parents would be there, but not a lot of other people. It worked so well we offered it to every family we thought had young children. Then we realized that relatives from away might want a place to relax between visiting hours, so we told our families: "Come and go as you want after the first viewing."

We also invited people who wanted to, to stay later in the evening. We changed our policy to sit down with the family after visiting hours, and go over the entire procedure for the next day: flowers, acknowledgement cards, car list and seating. It gave us a chance to remind families to bring the check for the clergyperson, grave opening, and others taking part in the service.

**Thomas Anonymous**

# CHECK OUT MY BOOK ON GRIEF FOR KIDS: HONEY THE ROCK HOUND
Trafford.com

**Eliminating the "welfare" (Pauper) casket. C + 10 = S x 100**

It started out as an emergency for us. We were serving a welfare family and had no welfare casket. We couldn't get one, or borrow one, so we used the next best unit we had. The body looked great, and the family was delighted—so much so, that we did the same thing the next time we had a welfare family. They didn't have to look "down" into the casket to see the body. That little bit of extra "fluff" made all the difference in the world. We chalked the extra cost of the better casket(which really wasn't very much at the time, maybe 10%)up to advertising and P/R. We got one heck of a return on our investment! We always embalmed the "welfare" body the same as we did any other body, and we treated that family as well as we did any other family. I made up a formula to represent what we had done. Here it is, "C" (cost of a welfare casket + 10% additional cost of next best casket) =100 times the satisfaction by the grieving family and the public.

## The Best Advice I Ever Received

. . . was from a guy who wanted to be a funeral director and couldn't get his license. It seems that this family wanted him to change the cosmetics on their loved one's body, and he wouldn't do it. Somehow the licensing board found out about the situation and denied him a license. The advice he gave me, that has helped me many times over the years was, "No matter how good you think the cosmetics are, if the family wants them changed DO SOMETHING! If necessary, just go through the motions, but do something!

Many times when the widow came in for the first time to see her deceased husband, I would ask her if his hair was combed right. Often I could tell there was a need for some adjustment, so I would go get a paper cup with some water in it, and a comb. With the widow standing there I would start making adjustments in the way the hair was combed. Often, I would put some water on the comb, and pass it to the widow. Being able to do the final adjustments with the comb often satisfied the widow. Again, it's the little things that make the biggest differences.

## Advertising And Public Relations
## What Worked, What Didn't

**The shift from advertising to public relations.** Pay your people to get out in the community and volunteer. Get everyone committed to ONE charity, or public service program, Pay the extras, like uniforms, if your guy is a Little League coach. Give them time off (with pay) to go volunteer at the soup kitchen. Pay someone's lodge dues if they like fraternal organizations. It may mean paying for a baby sitter. Pay everyone a little extra to shop at your local markets. They will cultivate personal relations over time, *and that's what will get you new clients, Those bucks are an investment.* Hire a cleaning lady to come in and do the dusting and heavy duty cleaning, while your people get out into the community, and patronize the coffee shops. Let your people know you expect them to be involved in one evening activity a week. You may have to pay for the baby sitter, but your people are cultivating relationships. Show them how the "Big U" strategy works. Encourage your people to get out and apply it in your community. Take your clergy(and spouses)to lunch. Do the same for cemetery superintendents, new business owners, florists. You have no idea(maybe you do) how precious those bucks are to the guy that's trying to hang on in a sluggish economy.

**Advertising items** are becoming more and more expensive. I suggest you limit items to a few nice pens. (Nothing will make someone cuss you quicker than if his pen that you gave him runs out when he needs it most.) Emery boards, a few safety pins, and some inexpensive plastic combs in the restrooms, communicate that you care. It may be too expensive just to leave them out now, but pretty plastic rain bonnets for the ladies always hit a home run. The last time we tried to get them, we could not. They are useful, inexpensive, and very much appreciated. A lot of bang for the advertising buck.

For a while we bought small packs of tissue, and left them around so a woman could pop one in her purse. We often tossed a couple packs in on the seat of a car that was going to the cemetery following a service. What about newspaper advertising? Large ads promoting something or other are, in my opinion, a waste of money. A small ad on the obituary page one or two days a week, consistently, week after week is more effective. I have seen very few television ads that I thought were tasteful for a funeral home. One was by a bank and would be appropriate for a funeral home. It had a picture of a stream of running water, in the woods, and some soft music playing. The voice said something like, "These few moments of beauty are brought to you by ____."

Another thing I have seen a few times, is a public service tribute honoring the police, fire department, Red Cross(for a blood drive, or following a disaster, etc.). The caption would read(in small print)this public service announcement sponsored by _____Funeral Home. If this were done one day a week, people would begin to look for it.

> Finally: Pay your staff more than "average", so they are not constantly looking for another job. Offer a generous profit sharing program. Reward excellence. Never criticize the one who makes an honest mistake. Remember the ones you made.

*There they are, your big guns, battle tested and ready to be deployed.*

Find one or two organizations in your community, that you really enjoy, and immerse yourself in them. Insist that everyone in your funeral home do the same. Everyone will be able to cultivate different RELATIONSHIPS.

Don't forget to pick up the tabs and chalk it up to advertising and P/R. I NEED TO SAY IT AGAIN. THERE IS NO BETTER WAY TO ESTABLISH SOLID, MEANINGFUL RELATIONSHIPS, THAN THROUGH THE FIVE PRONGED GRIEF RECOVERY PROGRAM. THIS NEXT CHAPTER IS JUST AN OVERVIEW. THE WHOLE PROGRAM IS SPELLED OUT IN DETAIL IN THE NEXT SECTION OF THE BOOK, "A CRASH COURSE IN GRIEF RECOVERY FOR SMALL GROUP FACILITATORS." THERE IS A SPECIAL SECTION THERE FOR FUNERAL DIRECTORS. AGAIN, DON'T FORGET TO GET IN TOUCH WITH ME IF **If YOU WANT HELP; THERE IS NO CHARGE.**

My desire is for this Grief Recovery Program to compel those of us in funeral service to place a lot more emphasis on "recovery" in the grief recovery equation than we have been. It will require a little more time at first, and a sincere desire to help grieving people, But isn't that what you want to excel at anyway?

This is a once in a lifetime opportunity to be out in front of the pack, to lead the charge, to point the way to a new concept.

## CHAPTER 6

# A GLANCE AT YOUR SECRET WEAPON

IT'S VERY DOUBTFUL THAT YOUR GOLIATH WILL BOTHER TO APPLY THE FIVE MINUTE RULE, OR ANY OF THE OTHER WINNING P/R STRATEGIES, OR TAKE THE TIME TO PUT A GRIEF RECOVERY STRATEGY TO WORK ON A LONG TERM BASIS, EVEN IF HE FIGURES OUT WHAT YOU'RE DOING. TAKE MY ADVICE. THESE THINGS WORK! YOUR HORIZON IS UNLIMITED. THE POTENTIAL IS THERE TO ELIMINATE A HUGE PERCENT OF GRIEF ALL AROUND YOU. AS YOU BLESS OTHERS, GOD WILL BLESS YOU. DONE CORRECTLY, THE PEOPLE YOU HELP GET RID OF THEIR LOAD OF GRIEF, WILL IN TURN REACH OUT TO OTHERS. THE BENEFITS FOR EVERYONE ARE ENDLESS.

**The Atomic Bomb saved the day for us in WW II.** It put an end to the fighting. It was our Secret Weapon. However, it also took planes to deliver the bombs; Naval vessals, guns, heavy artillery, tanks, thousands of commited men and women in uniform, and an entire nation behind them, to actually "win".

There's psychological warfare here too. Your secret weapon is absolutely no good until you and your staff are totally committed to using it faithfully. David's sling shot would have been useless, if he hadn't rushed the giant, deploying the projectile at the strategic moment. Besides that, the giant had left his face unguarded, and was totally unprepared for David's attack.

## Guard Your Integrity, It's Priceless!

Do you know what's being promoted at grief recovery support groups that you are referring your families to? Is it New Age philosophy, Eastern meditation, or blatant occultism? Why not offer *a complete grief recovery program* that you are comfortable with and that reflects *your* values, and receive the tremendous P/R advantages of offering such a program. The Crash Course In Grief Recovery takes you step by step through the entire process, from a thorough understanding of the recovery process, to organizing and facilitating all five prongs of the program.

## Your secret weapon is a five pronged grief recovery program.

## It could eventually affect everyone in your community for good!

Ideally, this is how the program is intended to work. It begins with two-on-one mentoring, for a newly widowed woman, when she's ready. The two mentors are widows who have worked through the grieving process, and can offer advice and support. After a few months with the two-on-one program, the widow will be ready to go into a small, facilitator-led grief recovery support group. This recovery process can take months, even years, for some to heal, but later, when she has worked through HER OWN grief issues, she will want to venture out again with some friends. This is where the widowed person's social support group is a blessing. It offers companionship, emotional support and social activities; oversees the other four phases of the grief recovery program; and offers a structure to accomplish worthwhile projects.

My desire is to compel those in funeral service to place a lot more emphasis on "recovery" in the grief recovery equation than we have been. It will require a little more time at first, and a sincere desire to help grieving people, but isn't that where you want to excel anyway? This is a once in a lifetime opportunity to be out in front of the pack, to lead the charge, to point the way to a new concept of grief recovery.

## The Grief Recovery Program

**This Is The Most Effective Public Relations Program Out There for funeral service professionals, barring none. For those who choose the program, this will become your secret weapon!**

If I climb up on my soap box and yell it to the high heavens, you probably won't listen, but Grief Recovery IS The Wave Of the Future. There is no other public relations program that will produce more return on your investment, period! You can't measure satisfaction, and you can't measure appreciation. This strategy will produce a superabundance of both, for you, and for everyone carrying a load of grief around with them.

**The five pronged grief recovery strategy** offers you the opportunity to make a major impact(for good), for many in your community, police and fire departments, veterans groups, hairdressers, churches, nursing homes, veterinarians (yes, pet owners grieve big time), and business and industry.

Because it will require some commitment, and extra time at first, it's doubtful that your Goliath will bother to do it. He won't have a clue about what's going on just like Goliath in the Bible. By the time your Goliath realizes what you have thrown at him, it will be too late. You will have gained the decided advantage. You will have moved on to the next phase of the program.

The five pronged strategy is not spelled out in order in the Crash Course In Grief Recovery section, but it's all there. Before you give up in despair, because it seems to be too complicated, trust me, it's not technical at all. It's not therapy, or counseling. It's just common sense, every day, down to earth "stuff" that gets results. It's lots more than a group of grieving people sitting around in a circle, feeling sorry for themselves. Anyone can grasp it. The whole thing may seem tedious, and unproductive, until one day you wake up and see some person who has previously been grieving, with a sparkle in her eye, a smile on her face, a spring in her step, and a renewed zest for life. At that point, you will have a whole new appreciation for what you have been doing. You will suddenly realize that this program can be compounded exponentially to benefit the whole community.

**The first thing that should be done** is to organize a widowed person's social support group. This is the easiest phase to accomplish. It gives an umbrella type of structure or covering for the other prongs, or phases, of the program. Everything is spelled out step-by-step in the next section of the book, and it goes into detail about how to structure the political framework to *your best advantage.* Without the social support group in place, the small grief recovery support groups will have to operate independently.

Over the years I have had many widows tell me that having a mentor during the first weeks of widowhood was very beneficial. This would be the number one priority for an outreach project for the social support group. After several weeks of two-on-one mentoring by other widows, the recently widowed woman will be ready for the small facilitator-led grief recovery support group. The whole process is spelled out in detail in the funeral director section of the last part of the book. Eventually the widow will have successfully worked through her grief issues, and is ready to move on with her life. That is when someone invites her to the social support group as a guest. That is not the end of the process.

## An Entirely New Type Of Support Group

When someone realizes for the first time that his or her loved one is actually going to die, and probably soon, they have a very difficult time dealing with the reality of it.(Sometimes I think it is the most difficult time of the entire grieving process.)This is when many people are told to set up a mortuary trust account, or get their funeral arrangements in order. It may mean admitting their loved one to an extended care facility, or nursing home. There are dozens of things that will need to be taken care of at the same time the person is grieving the most. It is at that time when a support group is badly needed. This is the new strategy that we have overlooked before, that could become the most effective public relations strategy in the book!

Because it is new, and has so much potential, don't slide over it. My first realization that there was a pressing need in this area was when I invited a friend, who was having difficulty admitting her mother to a nursing home, to sit in on a church support group. What she said to me next, changed my whole way of thinking in that area. "What I really wish you'd do," she said, "is start a support group for people who have to admit their loved ones to a nursing home." Well, I'm sure she is not alone in wanting support in that area, so here it is: a wonderful opportunity for funeral home owners to really help people during perhaps the most difficult time in their lives, and gain some valuable public relations advantage in the process.

Excuse me; but I need to say that if you go about this with the intention of helping many hurting people, and putting grief recovery principles to work, you will almost certainly succeed. It will fly because it is brand new, and the need is there. If you go at this with the intention that you are going to make a lot of money, and get the jump on the competition, it will come across as phony, and you will almost certainly fail at it. If you enjoy meeting new people, and new challenges, you'll enjoy setting up this new program.

I like to think of this new concept as a "C O P E" group, helping folks to cope with gut-wrenching problems. The strength of the groups will be the way hurting people will help each other. You definitely won't have all the answers at first, but you will enjoy finding the answers, and meeting the people who can help you.

You will need to identify what kinds of problems people in these situations face every day, so talk with those who come to you for pre-arrangements. Make an appointment with home health care agencies to talk about situations that folks have to deal with. Talk with social workers at nursing homes who deal with these issues every day. Some nursing homes even have groups that do this type of thing occasionally too. They will be great resource people.

*Suggestion: keep this strategy low—key (under the radar). A personal letter, or phone call, to those who have mortuary trust accounts with you; a blip in your holiday newsletter; and word of mouth for the time being, carry the ball. Be open about letting anyone into your group who is trying to cope with a loved one's serious illness.*

As these people work through their issues, eventually they will "get a handle on things," and move on. When the loved one does die, these people are ready for the two-on-one mentoring program(Chapter 6). After they have moved through that stage of the grieving process, they will welcome the small grief recovery support group at your funeral home, and within a few months to a year, they will be ready for the widowed persons' social support group.

If there is already a widowed persons' social support group in your community, go ahead and start the facilitator-led grief recovery support group. When those people are ready, encourage them to get involved in the other social support group in your community. Eventually, they may want to come back to you and start a social support group of their own.

I can't suggest when the grief recovery program will now be ready to take to the community: the churches, police, fire departments and veterans groups, etc. You will have make the decision as to when to do that. This is the fifth prong of your secret weapon.

To borrow a nautical term: batten down the hatches. There are rough seas ahead, but you are going to have a wonderful voyage seeing hurting people throw off the awful load of grief they are carrying. Tap into God's dynamic power source. He's given funeral service a wonderful opportunity. All we have to do is jump aboard, and ride the wave of the future! God Bless you.

If we are in trouble, and someone helps us, we instinctively want to return the favor. If someone has been carrying a load of grief around very long, and we help them get it off their back, words can't describe the gratitude and relief that person feels. They are always going to remember what you did for them!

**AS YOU REACH OUT TO YOUR COMMUNITY, HELP PEOPLE UNDERSTAND THE BENEFIT OF SUPPORT GROUPS. BE A HERO, TEACH GROUP LEADERS ABOUT GRIEF RECOVERY.** Help others become more effective as a leader. A million dollars worth of opportunity is sailing by your door while you snooze in front of the TV.

When does a small group become a grief recovery support group?

A N S W ER: When someone comes to the group with a serious problem, like a serious illness, loss of job, a miscarriage, broken relationship, parent child problems, addiction, or death of a loved one. Help others become more effective as a leader by teaching them about grief recovery

There is a section in the book that talks about the effectiveness of support groups.

**AS YOU REACH OUT TO YOUR COMMUNITY, HELP PEOPLE UNDERSTAND THE BENEFIT OF SUPPORT GROUPS. BE A HERO, TEACH GROUP LEADERS ABOUT GRIEF RECOVERY.**

A million dollars worth of opportunity is sailing by your door while you snooze in front of the TV.

# CHAPTER 7
# A CRASH COURSE IN GRIEF RECOVERY

## Section One

# Potholes in the Road to Grief Recovery

When I realized that the principles that apply to grief recovery following a death, could be applied to other grieving situations, I set out to get some support groups going at my church. I picked several women who I thought would be good facilitators and asked them to be part of my first group. Then I invited several others who I knew were dealing with gut-wrenching issues to join us.

I could not have picked a more diverse group of women personality-wise; however, within a few weeks they had bonded and felt comfortable enough with each other to let their hair down and talk openly about their problems. As we went along, I realized that each of the women that I wanted to be a facilitator had serious, unresolved issues from their past, that had not been dealt with. Until those situations were recognized and put to rest, they would be more focused on themselves than others in the group. This first group taught me several valuable lessons. People will disregard social and economic differences, if they are sincere about helping others, or if they are hurting badly themselves. It won't matter if the situations they are dealing with are different in nature: (death, divorce, family problems, etc.). People were helpful to one another and interacted spontaneously.

We had been meeting for several months when I found out, rather unexpectedly, that every one of the women in that group had experienced at least one miscarriage. None of them had sufficiently grieved their loss. What I saw happen, in the next few weeks, was nothing short of a miracle. Each of them was able, *with the help of the others,* to grieve the loss of their babies, complete their relationship with the lost child and move on. I was impressed with the intensity of their interactions and the way they bonded with each other. They all responded spontaneously and it was beautiful!

The women gave each child a name, shared their dreams and disappointments regarding each one, and told about the difficulties they experienced during their pregnancies. They planned to create a memorial garden at the church in the spring. They talked about planting flowers for each child and having a type of memorial service to say their goodbyes. It was heart-warming for me, to see the creative ways each one had chosen to express their feelings. They did not know the sex of the child they had lost, but they gave each one a name and brought in something that represented that child. For one, it was a pink ribbon for a little girl. For another, it was a tiny dress. One woman brought in a little toy for a baby boy. Each one had put a lot of thought into it and brought something.

When I suggested they pick a place in their home to create some type of memorial, several of them had already done so. When springtime came, they decided not to create their garden, or have a memorial service. They had all grieved sufficiently.

This is just one of the many tender, loving situations I've witnessed from different support groups, over the years. To me it was exhilarating. I can only imagine the pleasure you will experience when you witness this type of thing happening to you.

It won't matter whether you start out working with a group, or an individual, expect the unexpected. My hope is, that by the time you finish this book you will instinctively know in your heart when a person needs professional help. If you find yourself dealing with problems you aren't comfortable with, or feel qualified to handle, stop. Get that person professional help, ASAP! Be alert to the subtle ways grief attacks all of us. If we overlook abnormal behavior, it could spell disaster for the one grieving, as well as heartache for those who love him or her.

Don't let this discourage you. You will have a much deeper insight and be able to spot things that the average person won't recognize. People are crying out in pain. This book will give you the information you need to help them. I believe you are in this place, at this particular time, for a reason. I don't think for a minute it's an accident.

For years, my concept of a support group was any number of people, sitting around in a circle, feeling sorry for themselves. This book is focused on recovery—getting positive results and encouragement from your group.

Anyone with a servant's heart, *YOU*, can make a tremendous difference, just by helping family and friends around you. It will help you get the overbearing load of grief off people's backs. You'll learn how to apply every day, down to earth, common sense "stuff" that works. You'll thrill when you see people emerge from their grief with a smile on their face, a spring in their step and a renewed zest for life!

When I realized I was rapidly losing my vision, I woke up to the fact that **everyone** *with a serious medical problem is* *grieving!* There are all kinds of support groups for different medical conditions. I hesitated to mix people *with different* problems in the same grief recovery group. There just were not enough women with the same medical problem to start individual support groups. Yet, I felt they all needed a certain degree of support, right then. Eventually I decided to take a chance and mix them together, at least temporarily. The results exceeded my wildest expectations. I had proven to myself that the grieving process for someone with a medical problem is very similar to the recovery process for someone grieving the death of a loved one, or any other grief situation.

I was astounded to find that *all* the women were a lot more interested in scripture and prayer than I ever imagined. More on that later.

It was a unique group of women. One had recently been diagnosed with diabetes. I don't believe it was a coincidence that another woman in the group had suffered with it for years and became a close mentor to her. Two others in the group were battling fibromyalgia. The bonding between the two of them was absolutely remarkable.

As time went on, I witnessed many spontaneous acts of kindness and saw close friendships develop. Perhaps bonding developed a little more rapidly with those in the medically related support group than it did in other recovery groups. Generally, I think it depends on the needs of individuals and others becoming aware of the needs.

In most cases, if someone has gone through a full cycle with a support group, they are ready to read this material and help someone facilitate a new group. You will have a sixth sense about knowing when someone is not. If you are not sure, it's better to wait.

With God's help, you'll be able to make a big difference. Whether you're a high-powered human resource professional, or a Bible study leader, you will notice how easily the potholes we talk about next disorient and lure many of us into them.

**Do Not Charge Or Take Donations For Facilitating Support Groups, You Are Not A Therapist.**

## Potholes In The Road To Grief Recovery

*The first pothole we have to get around is fear.* It's the devil's most effective weapon. The more people fear, the more control he has over them. Many people are terrified of dying and they don't have to be. The twenty third Psalm in the Bible tells us that even though we walk through the valley of the shadow of death, God will be right there with us. Like a shepherd, He'll guide and comfort us every step of the way. We don't have to be afraid. Time and time again, in the Bible, Jesus tells us to "fear not." We have to work at it, but we can exchange fear for faith, which is of God and Jesus.

All things work together for good for those who love the Lord. (***Romans 8: 28)*** When the devil slams a door in our face, God flings open a window of opportunity. It may take us a while to find it, but I've seen it happen time and time again. If we trust God, He will always take whatever it is the devil throws at us and make *some* good come out of it! "Weeping may endure for a night, but joy comes in the morning." **(II Corinthians 4: 16-18)**

Fear allowed Satan to break through the hedge of protection God had placed around Job (in the Bible) and devastate him. **(Job 1: 10-11 and chapter 16: 9-14 in the Amplified version footnote explains what happened.)**

**Guilt: the *hidden pothole*.** *A* number of years ago when I was in the funeral business, a very prominent woman called and asked me to take her to a coastal community in down east Maine to bury her aunt's cremated remains. This woman was absolutely beautiful! The trip was going to take a full day and I have to admit, my thoughts were not one hundred percent lily white.

About an hour into the trip, as we were riding along talking, she said something that jolted me to the core and which I have never forgotten. She said, ***"The human soul cannot live with guilt."***

She was absolutely right. Guilt *can* literally *kill* people! Over the years I've witnessed several classic examples of it. The most striking was a woman with whom I was making a mortuary trust agreement. She and her family had cheated an insurance company out of a large sum of money and were putting some of it away for her burial.

While we were doing the paper work, I could see she was visibly shaken, as she made several references to the deception. I had not deposited her check, when her family called me. She had worked herself up into such an emotional state that she died.

Another situation affected me very personally. I worked closely with a woman to organize a widowed person's support group as well as several grief seminars in our area. She was having an affair with a much younger man when she was unexpectedly diagnosed with terminal cancer. I believe it was guilt that brought her to her death bed. Thankfully, she died in peace, after she accepted God's forgiveness.

You're probably thinking, what's *that* got to do with grief recovery? It has more than you can imagine. If someone carries around a load of guilt, it's going to constantly eat at their conscience and the devil won't give that person a minute's peace!

**Unforgiveness:** *the pothole we are most likely to get ourselves stuck in.*

Marcia saw her 12 year old son killed on his bicycle in front of her home by a drunk driver. For something like five years she harbored anger and unforgiveness toward the man. She told me that only after she went to his home, (she knew the guy) and told him she forgave him, did she begin to heal. She went on to have a wonderful ministry to other families in the area whose children had died.

If a person needs forgiveness themselves, remind them they can always receive it by bringing the situation to the Good Lord in prayer. Encourage them to do that anyway. He's always there waiting patiently for us to come to Him. He even knows our thoughts before we think them. **(Psalm 139)** Jesus talked a lot about un-forgiveness **(Beginning at Matthew 5: 22).** The point he emphasized was that we can't receive forgiveness for our own sins, if we harbor unforgiveness toward others.

**Picture an old jailhouse** with one window. There are only two bars in the window, and they are about two feet apart. (Plenty wide enough to step out between them.) One bar represents *fear*. The other *guilt*. Many in grief imprison themselves. They often "*fear*" things like finances, loneliness, especially during the holidays, the loss of relationships, and not being able to meet expectations placed on them. Instead of letting go and being everything they could be, they worry. Their greatest pain may be their own fear. The other bar represents things from their past. Things they feel they should have done better or differently. Couldawouldashoulda.

Some of us have had serious issues from our past that haunt us. **_There is absolutely nothing we can do to change the past!_** _We forget that, and tenaciously hold on to our guilt._

Once we have let go of fear and guilt, we still have to step over the window sill to be free. The window sill represents unforgiveness. A person is never free as long as unforgiveness is looming in front of them. Help others recognize these three culprits and walk away free.

**Being offended is a very dangerous pothole.** The Bible says "Don't be offended." Most of the time the thing that offends us is *not* intended to do so! We often misunderstand what is said. I remember getting a detention in high school because a teacher with a *serious* hearing problem completely misunderstood what I said to her. It's easy to take a joke the wrong way, too. Most of the time we get all pushed and bent out of shape unnecessarily.

**Jealousy is a pothole many of us unexpectedly skid into.** It's insidious. I suspect it works hand in hand with fear. If you recognize it in others, deal with it lovingly. The only way to combat it, that I know of, is through trust. If we find it lurking in ourselves, treat it like the plague. Many of the questions I suggest you ask a grieving person can be asked of someone you suspect is tormented with jealousy. It's possible the person doesn't even recognize it. Only after I was confronted, and made to realize what it was that tormented me, was I able to overcome it.

As a kid I was surprised when another boy picked a fight with me. He actually wanted me to beat him up so he would get some extra attention from his father. At the time, his dad worked for mine as a carpenter. Apparently the boy was jealous when his father talked about me.

**Resentment is a close cousin of jealousy and anger.** It takes a lot of self-control to steer around this pothole.

**Anger: It's the most dangerous pothole there is.** It's easy to get sucked up into anger, and it can take years for some of us to get out of it. Some people can't control their anger, and wind up in big trouble. I remember talking to one young woman in a group, who was told as a young child that her grandmother, who lived with the family, had gone on a trip. Actually she had died while the girl was in school. Years of pent up grief, denial, and anger were released within a few minutes that evening when she realized the truth. She expressed her anger at me, cried profusely, apologized "all over the place", for what she had said, and a little while later accepted me as a friend. It was a remarkable transition.

I believe anger *always* accompanies grief. Sometimes we're able to suppress it temporarily. Most often it comes out at the time of death. It can flare up when we realize for the first time that a loved one has a life-threatening illness. Medical professionals are particularly vulnerable as targets of anger when a family feels a serious illness has been misdiagnosed, or not recognized soon enough. Sooner or later anger comes out, often directed at God. You can be almost certain that anger is not directed at *you personally*. You just happen to be the first one to come along on whom they can vent their frustration. Say nothing, give the person a few minutes to think about what they've said or done, and they'll almost certainly apologize for it.

Some people explode when they get bad news. I had an appointment with a man once, who was absolutely rotten to me. As I was leaving his office he said, "Sorry I was so hard on you. Someone just mistook my dog for a deer and shot it."

Sometimes, as strange as it seems, people will be angry with (at) the person who has died, because they feel cheated out of something they wanted to do *with* them, or wanted the person to do *for* them. Don't let a grieving person's anger throw you for a loop. Encourage the one grieving to talk about their feelings-to say the things they need to say *to the deceased person*. That will begin the healing process.

A lifetime in funeral service taught me to be very cautious toward people who are "angry". Probably the hardest thing is to stay cool. Don't raise your voice, but don't back down either. Don't be offended. I've noticed that people who chose to be angry usually have an ulterior motive. Probably they are trying to get something for nothing. We of course, were always wary of someone trying to sue us for something or other. This became crystal clear when a family came to us after services for their loved one were over and said, in effect, "Everything was wonderful. We tried to find something to find fault with and we couldn't."

Usually I found people that were difficult to deal with at the onset, the ones with an attitude problem, were the ones to be extra cautious around and keep the guard up.

The first thing I learned about anger was, find something to agree about, anything. Take it little by little from there. Let 'em vent. Let the steam blow off in the whistle. Mirror their words back at them, "what I hear you saying is . . ." Say the same thing differently. Ask questions about why things were not satisfactory. Try to find out what's really "bugging" them. If there's a third party put everything on hold until the one making the complaint or accusation is eyeball to eyeball with the one presumably at fault or responsible for the complaint. Don't shoot from the hip. Be sure you have *all* the facts before making a final decision about the problem.

By all means don't tell them they "have" to do something. Them's fightin' words.

How far do you bend over backwards? Try and salvage the relationship without allowing the person with the complaint taking advantage of you. If you ask the person if they would "mind" doing something or other, you'll probably get a full frontal attack; "yes, I DO mind!" Be sure and thank the person for bringing the problem to your attention so you can "fix" it. Ask the person to suggest ways to help you so the problem does not happen again. I've seen rather contrary people become enthusiastic workers because someone got them involved in *"fixing"* the problem.

If a person threatens to do some irrational thing, ask, "What will that solve?" "How will that help?" "What will happen after that?" Let's face it, some people will kick if they're in swimming.

Know where to get help—whether it's calling 911, an emergency shelter, or crisis counseling. Also know which resources to tap into to solve problems, like prescription drugs, etc. Try and find out if a person who seems unusually upset or depressed may have forgotten to take their medications.

**Use of reverse psychology.** Sometimes a very negative person reacts positively to "reverse psychology." They've made their mind up, they're going to be contrary. Whatever the situation is, say JUST THE OPPOSITE of what it is you really want them to say or do . . . such as. "You wouldn't want to . . . . ?" "It isn't possible to . . . . ?" Sometimes a person will come around to your true position JUST TO BE CONTRARY! Be careful that the contrary person does not know exactly what it is you want from him or her. Use this as a last ditch effort. If they suspect what you are doing, the results may be worse than just plain *"no."*

**Betrayal** was probably the hardest thing in the world to accept, for the young woman I mentioned previously, who confronted me, more so, than her grandmother's death. The lesson is, *never try to protect children, or anyone else, by lying to them.* Sooner or later the truth will come out. Besides the grief, there will be pain and resentment. The whole grieving process will be compounded.

**Pity-party pothole.** I will likely get some flack on this, but some people actually *enjoy* wallowing around in their own self-pity! That person needs to be nudged into relationships, more than anything else. It's likely the person has no one they are close with. Others in the family probably don't understand the person's need for companionship. The person may be trying to find a way to grieve in an appropriate manner.

**Unlovely traits** are like potholes that we let ourselves slide into, from time to time. If our marriage partner develops some trait that simply bugs the daylights out of us, we can trade that person in for someone with *different traits*, or we could just love them for **who** *they are and overlook their unlovely traits.*

**"Wrong" feelings are like hidden potholes.** They can cause problems. People often feel guilty because they don't think they're supposed to have feelings of relief that a loved one has died. They may be angry because they have been shackled with their loved one's long term care and need to express their feelings. They are almost certainly emotionally drained. They may have felt robbed of their plans or deprived of certain pleasures. They may not have had the help they needed and harbor resentment. In most instances, taking care of a bedridden loved one becomes a real burden, a sacrifice. We can help that person sort out and express those deep emotions in an acceptable way. A support group would be wonderful for anyone recovering from this arduous ordeal. Show *much* love.

**The overly emotional person:** (Oops, I didn't expect that one.) You may come across a grieving person who has become overly emotional. Each time they meet someone who will pay any attention to them at all, they'll aggressively embrace them and weep profusely. They actually *enjoy* being stuck in that pothole! Try to get the person into a group. If you don't have one, talk to the person individually, or start one. If this does not improve in a short time, the individual needs professional help. *Always invite someone to go with you when working with an individual of the opposite sex!*

**Denial: These folks don't want to admit the pothole is there.** A grieving person may not be able to face reality. Some people in denial may refuse to view or touch their loved one in the casket. They may refuse to move their personal belongings. It's not unusual for them to set a place at the table for the deceased person. They may continuously dream of them, or talk aloud to them. They may insist the person appears and communicates with them. Try and have some family member or close friend around as much as possible, so the grieving person has someone to express their feelings to. Eventually this helps the grieving person with their denial. It's important for the grieving person to acknowledge the truth verbally. To *"say"* goodbye and anything else that they didn't get a chance to say *to the deceased person*, so they can complete their relationship. If the person is unable to accept or cope with the death in a reasonable time, they need professional help.

**Blame: The murky pothole.** One parent will sometimes blame the other in the death of a child. These folks have sunk "way in over their hub caps!" They're probably stuck in more than one pothole at the same time. Professional <u>**counseling will almost certainly be needed**</u>. *Sadly, many marriages end in divorce* following the death of a child. Try and plug the parents into some kind of support group. If there is none, start one yourself! One of the saddest things I've ever witnessed was a couple who had lost a child and started an amazingly successful parent support group in central Maine. For some reason, even they wound up divorcing.

**Disproportionately grieving the death of a child.** (I didn't expect that pothole to be so deep.) The death of a child can be a huge. Dads often try to work out their grief by throwing themselves into their job, or things like cutting grass and other physical activities. I've seen several moms mire themselves in this pothole and ignore their other children. Some seem to be emotionally needy. They just go on and on. I can't figure it out, except that *these mothers may be seeking attention from **other** people that* they can't get from their husband and family. Sometimes a grieving dad will not communicate with his wife, or anyone else. He just stuffs his grief. A parent support group would definitely benefit both of them. The problem in this situation is to get the dad to actually *go to* a meeting. Men seem to want to isolate more than women.

**Sainthood pothole:** Many parents can't see this one because their heads are in the clouds. They *want to believe* their child was a saint. Gently talk about childish pranks or naughty things the little one did. It will help the parents realize their child was normal. I stand in awe with this, because many of the children I have buried over the years were, in many ways, *very* "special". I'm groping like everyone else, with this.

**Grieving Children:** Children often feel responsible for situations they have no control over, for example: rejection, abuse, someone close to them moving, etc. Kids don't understand divorce and of course not death. Be on the lookout for anger, withdrawal and other emotional or behavioral problems. Get children to counseling fast, if you notice any of these problems developing. Encourage children to role play, draw and color things they can remember doing with the deceased person (or pet). Reassure a child that their actions did not cause a loved one's dying, any more than being good kept them alive. Some communities have programs for grieving children. Hospice may too. Any state mental health agency should be able to connect you (or a child's family) with professional help. Most therapists would know who to recommend.

**WASHOUT:** During a severe storm, sections of a road can wash out completely, and unsuspecting travelers can be in over their heads before they know it. On the road of life there is a major washout which can occur that will devastate us if we allow ourselves or loved ones to slide into it. We call it SUICIDE.

There are most often warnings such as depression, anxiety, stress or panic. Often a person isolates themselves. In most cases, BUT NOT ALWAYS, a person will talk about doing it. TAKE THAT PERSON SERIOUSLY! EVEN IF A REMARK IS DISGUISED AS A JOKE, OR A BACK-HANDED COMMENT!

Someone once described a person struggling with suicide as waking up every morning, feeling as if they had the worst case of flu imaginable and having no relief available. To them, suicide seems like the only way to find relief. I have seen it happen; when the person gave no indication at all they were contemplating suicide. In the instances I am aware of, there were underlying circumstances that loved ones failed to recognize. There were situations such as drug addiction, financial crisis or serious medical issues. In several instances it was very difficult to determine if the death was accidental or suicidal. One man tried to make his suicide look like a hunting accident. Others have intentionally run their car in front of a truck, or into a tree so it would look accidental. A man I had worked with closed himself in his garage and proceeded to work on the underside of his car with the motor running. Police are often confronted with someone who has a firearm *pointing at them. The person is forcing the officer to shoot them, instead of committing the act themselves.*

*At the first hint of a situation where suicide might be contemplated, get help! If a person seems to be in a daze, pay attention! Check out local Crisis Intervention, Community Services or the National Suicide Prevention listed in your phone book.*

**Post Traumatic Stress Disorder** is most often found with military people following combat. Police and sometimes firefighters may also experience it. It's more than a pothole. It's another washout! Some little thing will trigger a reaction. They'll have a flashback and relive some horrific incident. This requires a very special type of counseling to help the person suffering come to grips with the situation. It is my understanding of this type of situation, that the person has to work through the trauma before they can begin the grieving process. This is *very emotional and the person definitely needs professional counseling! Later on, a grief recovery support group may be appropriate.*

One excellent resource for families with a loved one suffering this way is "The Purple Heart Service Foundation P.O. Box 49 Annandale, Virginia 22003. Check out their website, "Purple Heart Society".

**Delayed grief:** Sometimes, following the death of a casual acquaintance, or some seemingly insignificant incident, a person will grieve way out of proportion to normal. They very well may not have been able to grieve sufficiently over some major loss in their past. It could have been the death of someone close to them. There could have been some trauma that they could not deal with at the time it happened. Some horrible thing from their past may still be unresolved. My own experience is a classic example.

My mother left my father for another man when I was very young, but it was not until I was a senior in high school, that I actually grieved my loss. A casual friend of mine was killed in a plane crash, and I grieved way out of proportion for that situation. It took me years to figure out that I was actually grieving the loss of my mother, as well as my friend, at the same time.

Here's something else that can happen. People are able to block bad experiences out of their mind. Sooner or later, some small, thing will trigger the painful memory and bring it to the forefront. Even though they will have buried the memory previously, they will have no choice but to deal with it right then! They may not even realize why they are so intense in their grief. There are some things you can do to help them work their way through the recovery process.

Let them "get it all out". Let them cry, rage, whatever. They may seem to have gotten over it, but it could crop up again any time. Offer them a glass of cold water and some tissues. Don't hurry the process. Try to help the person identify the root of each troubling issue. Treat each one separately. This may take weeks, or even months. These issues do not have to be dealt with in order, or within any time frame. It's easier if you can tackle the larger, more pressing issues first.

Review the questions and comments from chapter one and two. Many people have gotten stuck in more than one pothole. Help pull them out, one situation at a time.

**Loneliness:** the one pothole we can't get out of by ourselves. It can be awful. It is probably the number one reason to form support groups. There are complete instructions later on, regarding organizing and facilitating support groups. There are also many suggestions of things to do to avoid holiday depression. It doesn't take much to brighten someone's day. A phone call will do it.

**The Insidious Pothole:** can destroy everything that gets stuck in it. It tries to get everyone nearby to get stuck too. I'm talking about drugs and alcohol. People often use them as a crutch when the going gets tough. Several times over the years I have seen well meaning family members or friend give someone who is having a very difficult time dealing with the death of a loved one, some kind of medicine without checking with the person's doctor.

There may be a few moments when meds deaden the pain, or ease the pain, but sooner or later the person that's grieving so intensely has to face reality. They are better to have family and friends with them, rather than have the meds wear off in the middle of the night sometime, when no one is there with them. I once called a person's doctor and asked him about giving one of his patients something, because the woman was having such a hard time. The doctor refused to give her anything, because of what I have just stated. We tend to think we would never get stuck in one of these potholes ourselves, but it's easy to do. The trouble is, when we do get in one, we often sit there and spin our wheels, instead of seeking help getting out of it. It is my prayer that after you have helped grieving people claw their way up, out of the pothole they are in, you will go on and empower them to do the same thing for others.

**There's no end to potholes** that can prevent us from healing. Here are a few more that are very apt to appear unexpectedly: losing our temper, condemning or criticizing others, having malice in our hearts, meanness, contentiousness, snobbishness and arrogance. We need to reassure grieving people that their feelings of fear and worry, depression, resentment, guilt, bitterness, woundedness, anger, hostility, abandonment and feelings of having been cheated are all normal and part of the grieving process. It's when we allow ourselves to be overcome with these feelings and obsess over them, that we need help. With love and patience, *you* can help most people work themselves out of these potholes and receive a great deal of satisfaction doing it. It's an exciting road we're on together, in spite of all the potholes.

## Section Two

# Understanding Grief

Do you remember the first time you had a crush on someone of the opposite sex? I was rejected by my first heart throb in first grade and it hurt right on into Junior High. Do you remember when all of your friends were invited to someone's party and you were not, or when somehow you didn't quite fit in with the kids you wanted to be friendly with? Did you ever hear something like, "You aren't as smart as your sister is" or, "you'll never amount to anything." Do you remember when you first realized your report card wasn't as good as some other kids' and they taunted you because of it? These things leave lasting scars on our minds and we grieve for years, because of them.

As we get older, there are everyday situations when we grieve too. The job "we'd die for" goes to someone else, nowhere near as well qualified. We grieve for many different reasons. Some examples are: loss of a sibling, loss of a coworker or friends; job loss; moving to or from a community; loss of a home by fire or; foreclosure, retirement or serious health conditions.

Here are some other issues you may encounter in your grief recovery support groups: People ending romantic relationships, divorce; sexual abuse; parental abuse; death, or serious medical issues regarding a child, spouse, parent, relative, or close friend. Something not often mentioned is miscarriage. See chapter 1. You will likely have folks in your groups dealing with *personal* medical problems. Their grief is as painful as the death of a loved one.

Parents mourning the death of a child should be in a group by themselves, to begin with. More on this later. In the first chapter, we talked about potholes in the road to grief recovery. We usually slide into them without realizing it, but bounce right back out. It's when we get stuck in one that we need a little help. It's not abnormal for someone experiencing the death of a loved one, to ask, "Am I losing it?" A week or so later they'll be fine. With the help of this material you'll be able to reassure most people that "this too shall pass."

**Letting Off Steam.** Most kids today will never experience a huge locomotive letting off steam in a train station. Not many of them have seen a pressure cooker either, or even a tea kettle. Grief is like steam. It builds up inside us. If we can't get rid of it in an acceptable way we "blow up"! Everyone seriously grieving needs to be able to let off steam, get rid of the pressure. They need affirmation that they have done the best they could under the circumstances and have reacted normally. Keep in mind that medical conditions, abnormal behavior, and serious emotional problems sometimes result when people are unable to grieve and let off steam.

The *big secret to grief recovery, the key, the bottom line, is to help the person grieving complete their relationship with the one who has died, or caused the pain: to* help them sort things out and work through unresolved issues. You will have a *gut feeling, a quickening in your spirit,* when someone needs professional help. Be alert to it. If you do detect abnormalities, or quirks in people's behavior, following a crisis, you'll be right there to help them connect with the professionals.

With so much happening at once, and the emotional turmoil it's created, people often wonder if they are "losing it". They will probably need help sorting everything out in their own minds, by knowing that others care and will be there for them, helps a lot. Support them as they tie up as many loose ends as possible. Help them sort out the different factors contributing to their grief. It's vitally important that if there are unresolved issues, they **make amends, *if possible*, and *forgive*.** Ask them if they would rather be right, or happy. If they need you to go with them to resolve an issue, by all means, do it. If *they* need forgiveness, and the person they have been involved with has died or moved, encourage them to take the issue to God in prayer.

**Stages of Grief**: Nearly everyone goes through pretty much the same processes or stages of grief following the death of a loved one. The process is similar if they have experienced serious loss, or survived a crisis. The "stages" of grief don't always happen in the same order or intensity. Being able to recognize them will be helpful to you.

**Whamo! The first one is usually** *Shock: like* a hit beside the head with a baseball bat, or a punch in the gut! Close behind is **Denial:** Could this be a night-mare? I'll pinch myself and find out. This is where **bewilderment and numbness** overtake many of us. Sometimes these last for several days. The person often needs help to sort things out. **Warning: don't leave a seriously grieving person alone to do any task that is in any way dangerous. People in shock are often bewildered even if they don't show it. THEY DO NOT FUNCTION NORMALLY. THEY SAY THEY'LL DO SOMETHING IMPORTANT AND**

## FORGET THEY EVEN SAID IT. THEY WALK AROUND IN A DAZE!

Try and have someone **stay with** a person who has just experienced the death of a loved one, or who has just gone through a traumatic experience. Offer to call a close friend, neighbor or relative to come and stay with them. Help them sort things out, but don't hurry the process. It will only confuse them more. Just being there, reassuring them that they can get through the ordeal, and others will be there for them, is more helpful than you can imagine. **DON'T GIVE THE PERSON ANY NON-PRESCRIBED MEDICATION.** Sooner or later they will have to deal with the reality of what's happened. Better to do it with someone with them, then later when they are alone and the effects of the drug wears off. Just a drink of cold water works wonders, especially if someone is crying hard. A cool damp cloth on their face, or back of the neck is also soothing. Often when facing a serious illness or impending death, people will try to **bargain with God.** (See chapter six). Prayer changes things, *but you don't bargain with God*. He knows us better than we know ourselves.

*Anger*: *Everyone* coping with grief goes through it at one time or another. My anger was at God, because I didn't think He answered my prayers for healing. Unfortunately, sometimes potholes get in the way of answered prayer and healing.

**Loneliness:** After services for a loved one, family members return to their routine. Many family members live some distance away from each other, so often there is little long term support. The nights, or an empty house to come home to after being away or working, makes a compelling argument for a support group that I know of. Chapter six goes into detail on how to organize and facilitate different groups for different situations. In the meantime, reach out to those who are lonely. I've seen a number of families shield an elderly parent when their spouse dies. If the person can understand, they need to be very much involved in the decision-making process. *Don't shut them out!* Let them grieve. Remember the betrayal pothole.

**Helpful Things To Talk About.** Use this outline when working with an individual in grief, or to facilitate a grief recovery support group. ***Don't rush the process.*** The more anyone can express their feelings the better. Take your time talking about each one of the items, *with each individual* in your group. Try to stay on one subject until everyone has talked through it thoroughly. Come back to each person more than once. Put the time factor out of your mind. Mirror people's words back to them for clarity and to allow the grieving person to hear what they have said. **Stay emotionally "tuned in"**! Once anyone thinks you have distracted, or not **completely connected**, you've "*lost them*", and probably the rest of the group too!

* Tell me about your loved one.
* What hobbies did he or she like?
* Was there one favorite time or experience that you had together?
* What accomplishments of theirs do you feel good about?
* Were there other accomplishments that were less significant?
* What things did he or she enjoy most?
* Where was his or her favorite place?
* Did he or she have a favorite song? Play it.
* A favorite poem? Read it.
* Bible scripture? Share that.
* What did he or she do for work?
* How did that affect your life together?

* What things happened in their life that were traumatic?
* Serious illness, parent or child's death, job loss, moving?
* Tell me about their childhood, education, military service?
* Did they have strong feelings about religion, politics etc.?
* When did you become aware of the seriousness of your loved one's illness?
* When did he or she? How did they react to the news?
* Did they want to talk about it? Was it difficult? Did it help?
* If not, do you wish you had talked about it more? Why didn't you?
* Tell me about the treatment? Did it help? Was it painful?
* Did you discuss the treatment with your loved one? Talk about their condition just prior to their death. Were there medical things you didn't understand? That they didn't?
* *It's extremely important for the person to know that they did everything possible to help the deceased recover. If they couldn't, they need reassurance that they did everything possible to make them comfortable their last days.*
* Closure: Are there things you wish you could have said to your loved one that you didn't get chance to say?

IN YOUR MIND'S EYE, PICTURE THE PERSON HERE IN FRONT OF YOU. NOW SAY THE THINGS YOU NEED TO SAY TO THAT PERSON.

### Are There things beyond "I Love You," that you need to say?

Talk about your feelings of fear, worry, sadness, resentment, anger, guilt, bitterness, hurt, hostility, abandonment, or being cheated. We need to identify these emotions (potholes) and talk about them. Think of it like going to the dentist. A few minutes of discomfort versus long term benefits.

**Talk about everything** regarding the funeral or memorial service decision making and how the process helped you. Talk about community support and bonding throughout the process. Try to get the group to **talk about *one thing at a time*.** "How do you feel about such and such?" "That particular situation must have been awful!" "Were you afraid?" "Did it make you mad?" "How did your loved one react?" "Were you able to resolve the situation?" "Could you talk about it afterward?" "Did it help?" "Was there forgiveness?" "Emotional healing?" "Are you stronger because of it?" Repeat their words and then pause. ("mmmmmm".) "I'll have to think about that." "\_\_\_\_ tell me how you dealt with that," "Amazing." "Incredible." Don't imply you don't believe what they say. Repeat the words and just shake your head. Say "Wow." "My goodness." or something similar. "Did you have anyone to talk with about that?" "Did they understand?" "How did talking with the person help with \_\_\_\_?" Invite others in your group to get involved.

In a group setting, try to draw everyone there into the conversation, especially those that let others do all the talking. "What do you think about *that* Jane?" "Have you ever had a similar situation, Mary?" "Could the situation have been resolved in a different way, Pauline?"

**If you have someone who has a hard time opening up,** try to get them to share something like . . .

"Tell me Mrs. Jones, did your husband ever Bar-B-Q?"
Answer: "No".

Q: "Did he ever cook a meal for you?"
A: "No".

Q: "When you went camping did he ever cook over the campfire?"
A: "Well, . . . yes, we were at state park once in 19 and he cooked burgers for the kids."

Q: Did the kids ever talk about their father cooking the hamburgers?"
A: "No."

Q: "Tell me about your husband's hobbies?"
A: "He didn't have any."

Q: "He didn't have _anything_ he enjoyed doing in his spare time?"
A: "No."

Q: "Did he have a garden?"
A: "Oh yes, he raised all our potatoes."

Q: "He must have been a pretty good gardener to do that."
A: "Yup, he grew a lot of carrots and string beans too."

Q: "Were you able to can any beans?"
A: "Oh yes my husband worked with me to get the beans snipped and cut up for canning."

Try this: Ask, "Why is it?" repeat what the person has just said but asked as a question. Or, say, "I like that. You mean?" and repeat what the person has just said, using a few different words. Say something like, "I hear what you're saying—you think . . ." repeat what they just said. Or, say, "Do you think that . . . ?" (Repeat what the person has just said, differently.) "Would be a good solution?" Often you can draw a person out by expanding on what they have just said. Be careful that the shy person doesn't think we are "bugging" them or picking on them to talk. It takes some people a long time to get comfortable enough around other people to be willing to say *anything*. That's why you don't want to open the group up to newcomers after a few weeks.

Sometimes just pairing two people off at first and having them talk about their loved ones works better than getting them to open up in a group. Ask them to share with the other person some of the "special" qualities their loved one had. "What's the fondest memory you have of them?" is a good place to start. Give them things from the guidelines above to talk about.

In the case of a divorce, the grieving person usually paints the one that wounded him or her in the worst possible light. Spend time on how they coped with day-to-day problems. What helped the most?" "What was the most difficult to deal with?"

Have them talk about when the relationship started to fall apart. When did they first suspect things were heading for collapse?" "What efforts did you make to salvage the relationship?" "What effort did the other person make?" In this case, the trick is to get the person who's grieving to admit that there must have been some good qualities about the other person. Otherwise why did they love them to start with? Until true forgiveness takes place, I'm convinced the wounds won't heal.

I have learned that you can include people dealing with different situations in most support groups. My experience has been, that regardless of what people are struggling with themselves, they are willing to accept others in, so they can receive help too. Consider inviting people with different grief-related issues to join your group. Do not mix men and women, period. Consider people who are dealing with death or separation from a "significant other." Be alert for parents of kids hooked on drugs, or in trouble with the law, and parents of teens who are soon to become parents themselves.

Realize that anyone dealing with these situations is grieving intensely! I see a real need for support groups for adult children forced to place a parent, or other family member, in a nursing home. Many of these people are grieving a lot more than many of us realize. Nursing homes, funeral homes or churches should be offering support groups for these people. However, if there is no group available for them, invite them into one of your groups. Or let them help you start a group.

Carefully consider support groups for families of incarcerated felons. This requires special sensitivity, but the need is certainly great. Do not try to get this type of group started without having some experience with other groups. Another thing few of us think about is the death of someone's pet. To many, especially the elderly, a pet is a family member and treated accordingly. There are some suggestions for support groups for grieving pet owners. There is not a lot of difference between grieving the loss of a pet, that one interacts with every day and a casual friend or distant relative that has died. I would ask you to be alert and sensitive to the feelings and hurts of the elderly and children.

**Very soon now,** you will be equipped to facilitate any group. We'll get more specific later. Some issues are so unique, (like abortion, or working with the family of someone incarcerated), that those grieving should be dealt with in a separate group. If it's a critical issue, consider working with just one or two people.

**<u>Always</u> have another helper or support person with you!** It could be a member of the person's family, or the widowed person's support group.

You will` have to step out of your comfort zone when you decide to get involved. When you see anyone hurting, find out if they would like to be part of a support group with similar issues. When anyone is trying to cope with a problem, knowing how someone else dealt with the same issue can be very helpful. In many cases, just having someone to talk with is wonderful. You will find it very satisfying to put a group together, watch them bond and work through their issues. Wonderful things always happen. This was evident when a single woman in one of my groups wound up in the hospital. Words can't describe how delighted I was to see the rest of the group respond in love. They checked her home, fed her three cats, brought meals to her when she returned from the hospital and chauffeured her until she was ready to drive her own car again. Close friendships extended way beyond the life of the group. Now, with this information, you have a wonderful opportunity to serve others who are hurting. Always remember, you are not alone. **Hebrews Chapter 12 verse 1** in the Bible talks about the great cloud of Saints in heaven, observing our every move. It's like a giant sports arena, full of cheering fans at a ball game. We just can't hear or see them cheering.

**Please don't try to do any** counseling, or therapy. You'll be in over your head! That's for the Christian psychotherapist or pastor to do. This book will teach you **every day, common sense, down-to-earth "stuff" that will really help people who are grieving.** It will give *you* an understanding of some of the things to be aware of so you can refer them to the professionals if need be. The sooner someone who needs it gets help, the greater the chance of their recovering. Refresh your memory, take another look at the potholes in chapter one.

**Caution: Know who it is that you can refer people to for Christian counseling or therapy.** Not all clergy people are Christian. If they do not believe that Jesus was the son of God, or that God did raise him up from the dead; and that the Bible is the final authority and rule book, and if they do not know the difference between right and wrong, **DON'T REFER ANYONE YOU KNOW TO THEM!**

**Your First Meeting:** Invite everyone there to consider their friends who are grieving, and invite them to attend the next meeting with them. Set a time limit of not more than a month for bringing in new members. After that, it will be like starting over. I've found that people in a support group will bond very quickly, and start sharing personal things with each other, but when someone new joins the group they will not do it until they feel comfortable with, and *trust* the new person. One of the first things you should do is **assure confidentiality**. It's essential, and it's nice to remind everyone from time to time that **what they say will not go any further**.

Ask everyone to share what it is they want to gain from the group and what their expectations are. I like to remind my groups that I have expectations too. I expect each of them to become a facilitator—to feel the satisfaction and pleasure of seeing others emerge from meetings with **a sparkle in their eyes, a spring in their step, a smile on their face and a renewed zest for life!**

Women often know how to get a grieving person talking. In setting the groundwork for your first group, tell them that they will know how to get beyond the just-talking stage. They'll learn how to help anyone else get out of the potholes and complete their relationships in an acceptable way—to get back on the road of life. **The possibility of empowering others to do good has never been greater.**

Be vulnerable yourself. Let them know how you got to be where you are, and if you have any personal grief issues, be willing to share them with your group. They'll respect you for it.

You may have an agenda all planned for a meeting, get there, and find out someone has something altogether different that they really need to talk about. It could pop up in the middle of a conversation. Be willing to bend. People will not *really engage* with you (or anyone else), as long as they have personal issues that are gnawing at their insides.

To be effective, you have to *really* love the people, and want to help them work through their pain. Don't hurry the process. Let everybody "get all talked out" on each topic. Don't hesitate to come back to the same topic again and again, if someone wants to talk about it. Ask everyone if they have any questions, or if you have made yourself clear on whatever it was you talked about. If someone has anything that is "bugging" them, or if they have ***anything*** on their mind, let them talk it out. If someone has any kind of issue, they need to have an opportunity to completely deal with it. Everyone ought to be assured that if anyone has something bothering them, they are free to talk about it, and get it at least brought out in the open. They will *not completely* engage in group discussions as long as they have pressing issues themselves. Get others" input before moving on. Get every issue talked out. If someone is absent, when you discuss an important subject, discuss it with the others, wait a couple of weeks, and come back to the issue again, after everyone has had time to mull it over. Forget any kind of a timeline for covering topics, or winding down a group. If folks need to continue the support group, *they'll find the time and a way to do it. If strong bonds are developing, encourage them to continue on with the group socially.*

I go over all of this later, but let me mention it here, too. Don't try to set any time limit for anyone to talk, or have any specific rotation of who talks when. Encourage everyone to be spontaneous. I remember one very meek woman in a parent support group who got fired up and dominated the conversation for most of one evening. She was *very* passionate about what she needed to get out. Once she said what she needed to, she backed off for the rest of the time the group met. If someone continues to dominate the conversation for more than a week or so, get them off by themselves and *ask them to help you get others in the group more involved in each conversation.*

Encourage everyone to bring in poems, Scripture readings, or other things that are meaningful to them. In one group, dealing with medically-related issues the women felt so strongly that I was not being spiritual enough. They decided to alternate between themselves each week, and lead the discussions. I sat in awe as times they would point out, focus on, and shine an entirely different light on a familiar passage of Scripture. They each committed to pray for one another by name every day.

Chapter 5 is all about God, the Bible, and answers to tough questions. Many people don't have a clear understanding of what the Bible has to say about some of the issues. Some of them (me included) were, or are, mad at God. That's one reason I want you to read the whole book before you start a group. Like anger, at one time or another, nearly everyone who is grieving questions God. Why do bad things happen to good people? Is my loved one going to heaven? Am I? What about little kids? Do we die and then come back as some other animal? Will I see my pet in heaven? Do we sleep first and then rise up on the last day? These issues are all covered, and where to go in the Bible to check it out yourself.

**How long should I keep a support group going?** You will know when a group has reached the end of it's life. Each group has it's own life cycle. One group may meet for only a few weeks and for whatever reason the participants drop off one at a time. If that happens, invite each one from that group to sit in on the next group whenever it starts, and the next one after that. Continue doing that for at least six months until each person has found a group they're comfortable with. Some people have a great deal of difficulty being in a group of any kind. Don't give up. You'll develop sensitivity to just how long to engage. People may be embarrassed to get too intimate with people they don't know yet. Invite anyone to bring a friend. Just be sure the friend is willing to "ride it out" all the way. Be absolutely positive that they and the person who brings them, understand the confidentiality rule. Then you can engage them just like everyone else in the group. You may be surprised to find out that the friend has unresolved grief issues they are dealing with too.

# Abandon Ship

Don't be surprised if someone that seems to be doing well suddenly comes up to you and tells you they are no longer going to be attending your support group. (Either that, or they just don't bother to show up.)

**Don't take it personally!** Chances are very good that they are stuck fast in one or more potholes. (Chapter 1)

What I have found is, that very often the person is not willing to deal with their own grief issues. Most of the time, my experience has been that the person was not willing to forgive someone from their past. Even when they knew very well what they should do to be free from the burden of grief, they would rather be "right" than happy. Anyway, tell the person you will be willing to talk with them anytime over the phone. The next time you start a group, invite the person to join you. Once again, don't take it personally, if they say no again. Pray that the person will find peace, and resolve their issue with God's help. That's all I know of to do. I am willing to talk with you, as long as I am able. Contact me by Email. **pointtheway@myfairpoint.net Tom**

## Section Three

# Family Issues

By now I'm sure you recognize that many family issues are really someone getting stuck in one or more potholes. If someone needs your help, it's good to have an understanding of the problem ahead of time. Here are some grief issues you may be confronted with, where a little more background could help you a lot.

The more you understand every facet of a grief-related problem the better you can help the one grieving sort things out. Mirror their words back to them. Encourage them to make amends, seek forgiveness and, if possible, resolve every issue. Bring up the subject often. Some things have to be discussed again and again. If they need to say things *to* another person, try to make it happen. Would it help to offer to go with them while they do it? Help the person work through the issues that can't be changed. Offer hope and encouragement. Just letting someone know you are concerned and will reach out in love means everything. Walk with them the extra mile. The Bible says "Blessed are the peacemakers, for they shall be called the son's (or daughters) of God." **Matthew chapter 5: verse 9.**

People tend *not* to talk to someone grieving about their deceased loved one. We should do just the opposite. We should bring up those precious memories, calling him or her by name. One particular lady I knew drew much comfort from a story I shared with her about her deceased husband. He was Postmaster in a small Maine town. Each year the Road Commissioner came and asked him to point out where a particular manhole was positioned under the ice and snow, on the road out in front of the post office. The fact that the postmaster could point to it precisely from his office window gave his widow great pride. Hearing about it gave her much comfort. **Little things mean a lot.** Share those memories with others. My experience has been that once I helped anyone get that load of grief off their back, a close *bond developed and* they became a fast friend. I believe the same will happen for you.

If any type of memorialization or service took place for a loved one, it should be discussed in detail with the group—*every*thing about it—what they liked, what they did not. What was meaningful, what people said, what the clergyperson did and said, ***everything.***

**Parent Support Group**: Very often parents will divorce after the death of a child. I have even seen it happen *when both parents together ran a grief recovery support group*! Time and talking seem to be the only healing ingredients, other than counseling. Your role is to be sure parents have closure with the deceased child and complete relationships.

Don't rush the process. There'll be a good night and a week or so a parent will lose it! Have a ***tissue box and the ice water*** handy. Be gentle, be loving, and be ready for the ***LONG*** haul.

Teens tend to be rebellious and their death may follow an argument or disciplinary maneuver. Watch out for self blame. Even more devastating, is one parent blaming the other for the child's death. Remember, forgiveness is the only "real" cure. Healing won't start without it. It needs to sink into their heads that there is nothing anybody can do about the past. It's over, now work on forgiveness!

**With the death of a child,** I found a lot more anger at God and hard questions in this area. See chapter five. If you need help, find a Christian Psychotherapist or Pastor. Don't hesitate to invite parents whose children died several years ago to meet with you. There's a very good chance they never had closure with their child. If they did, they may be ready to help others. I found that parents of deceased children often know of other parents in nearby communities they can invite to meetings. For someone that needs help, an hour's drive is no problem.

We've learned that we have to deal with anger. Its part of the grieving process and it always manifests itself sooner or later, (sometimes years later). Anger and unforgiveness usually go together. They're like pet rocks. Remember that craze? We carry them around, weighing us down. Eventually we have to drop them. Get rid of them; bury them, throw them in the ocean or over a cliff. For some reason we like to go back and pick them up again. Many churches have a ceremony where people will actually lay a rock at the foot of a cross, representing taking our cares to Jesus. He has offered to carry *all* our burdens (rocks) for us.

In a support group, try to get to the "root" of the problem. Then help that person deal with it. In the back of your mind remember that a grieving person may be stuck in two or more potholes at the same time. Deal with just one issue at a time. If it's a sin issue, the person needs forgiveness. If it's unforgiveness, they won't heal until they completely let go of the resentment. If there has been a fractured relationship, it's much better to go to the person and make amends. If that's not possible, it helps to write a letter to the person, share it with others, and in the case of a deceased person, take it to their grave, out in the woods, or down back- anywhere and "bury" it.

**Suicide**: Usually the suicide victim has indicated previously that they are contemplating going through with it. The trouble is, others don't take them seriously. Help a family get in touch with the American Federation for Suicide Prevention.

Their website is **www.afsp.org They have resources available if you want to delve into this area further.** However, to get started, just follow the guidelines in chapter two. Google "Suicide support groups," for more resources.

To me, suicide is the most selfish, despicable act any person can inflict on anyone that loves them. If anyone doing it could realize the anguish and pain they are causing, they would certainly not do it. The problem is, I'm wrong! I once heard an expert on suicide tell her audience that many people contemplating suicide wake up every morning feeling like they have the worst case of flu imaginable. And **she said** *they have no relief*! They are tormented day and night. **That indicates to me that there could be demonic influence driving the person.** I have often been told by families of victims that their loved one was constantly compelled to find drugs or some other means of accomplishing their objective. Some people with terminal illness want to avoid the excruciating pain and suffering, or spare their family impoverishment. We need to take the advice of the old Indian who declared that we can never understand another person until we walk in their moccasins for the full cycle of the moon. If a husband or wife is the survivor, work with them one on one for a while. BE SURE OTHER FAMILY MEMBERS ARE AROUND, OR TAKE SOMEONE WITH YOU! *Never* work with another person (outside of your immediate family) in any kind of grief recovery work, alone!

**Later on, try and involve others in the family for a long term family support group. It's my opinion that there are so many gut-wrenching issues that are unique and different regarding suicide, that other people in a group, not having experienced them, would be very uncomfortable with them and likely leave the group.**

**Suicide of a child.** Over the years I've organized and worked with several grieving parent groups, **but never** for parents of a suicide victim. If you see a need, don't hesitate. Do something. **Something is better than nothing**! I believe God has placed this material in your hands so you can use the knowledge to help others. You do not have to look very far to find hurting people.

Parents going through this awful trauma need community support. They need to know they are loved and their child is loved by the community. This may be a time when parents try to isolate. Don't let them, if you can possibly stop them. If they are adamant about not having a service, offer to "just get together" with family members and talk about their loved one. It would be similar to an informal Life Appreciation Service, only very low key. One suggestion would be, after the family has agreed to do this (and it may be months down the road), have them ask everyone who comes to the get-together, to either bring something to represent the one that has died, or to write out some good things they remember about the person and share them. You ***should not*** mix parents of suicide victims with other grieving parents! Each situation will of course be unique. I can imagine a situation with parents of a child who died from an illness, being acquainted with the parents of a suicide victim, and wanting to reach out to them. That might work. My experience has been that most grieving parents are very self centered. They are just not ready to reach out, and won't be for a very long time.

**I DON'T THINK CHILDREN REALIZE THE FINALITY OF SUICIDE. THEY ARE SELFISH, ANGRY, AND THINK THAT PERHAPS THIS WILL HELP THEM GET THEIR OWN WAY.**

I recommend that you work with just one set of parents at a time, Let them know you are available anytime they want to talk. Knowing who other parents are who are trying to cope with the suicide of a child can give them the opportunity to establish communications with one another—someone they can call when they're having a really bad time. After both sets of parents have worked with you for a month or so, get them together *if they both agree.* Let each couple know the location and phone number of the other. Let them contact the other parents if they want to, but I don't recommend that you get them together for a meeting at first.

**Caution: What may be rumored as a suicide could be an accidental death due to some unknown factor. The child may be fantasizing not really intending to go through with it, not realizing how dangerous whatever it was he or she was doing really was. So when things get intense and emotional, explore that possibility with the survivors. Do this only if you have doubts yourself.**

These principals of grief recovery also apply to a family dealing with an adult suicide. Use every ounce of love you have working with them! Undoubtedly there will be a great deal of guilt. Review chapter one. God bless you.

**The Death of a Pet:** I'll never forget Horace. (Not his real name.) He was one of the nicest guys I've ever met, like an oversized Teddy bear. He was the kind of a guy everyone wants to hug. Horace's son was killed somewhere out west working in the mountains. At the same time his wife was dying of cancer, and within a few months of their son's death, she went to be with him. Horace was like a rock. I don't remember seeing him even cry.

Then one day he came into the office. He was weeping profusely, red-faced and just having an awful time. I thought he was going to "blow a gasket." His dog had died. Since the death of his wife, he had taken it with him in his truck, everywhere he went. It was his constant companion. I remember thinking, "That's strange, the guy thought more of this dog than he did his wife and son." But that was not the case. The dog's death was devastating to him, but what Horace was really doing was grieving the loss of his son, his wife and his dog, all at the same time. A classic example of delayed grief.

Yes, people do grieve the death of their pets. And the more attached they become to them it seems, the more they grieve their loss.

**Will I See My Pet In Heaven?** That question must have perplexed pet lovers forever. Solomon talked about the spirit of man and the spirit of animals going to the same place. **Ecclesiastes 3: 9-21 & 12-7**. Just as there are children in heaven, I feel certain there are pets there for them to play with, too. The Bible says that in the end times a child will safely play with poisonous snakes and the lion will lay down with the lamb. Revelation talks about horses.

Probably the most clear Scripture on it is in **Psalm 49 verse 12**. "He (man) is like the beasts that perish. James tell us

**(chapter 2, verse 26** that apart from our spirits our bodies can do nothing. If this is true for us, I believe it's also true for animals. Their spirits go to be with God. Their bodies go back to dust. Jesus told us that not one sparrow falls without God knowing and caring. **Matthew 10: 29.** When we are asked if we will see our pets in heaven, I believe we're on solid ground to answer *YES*.

There is a heartwarming story from the internet, about two little boys that liked to play with toy horses. One of the boys became terminally ill with cancer, but the two boys were still able to play together occasionally. One day, shortly before the little guy with cancer died, he was overheard asking his friend, "Do you know if there are horses in heaven?" "I don't know," the other boy replied, "I sure hope so!" The little boy with cancer died soon after that. The other boy's mother did not want to tell her son at first, but eventually she did tell him his friend had died. "I know, mom," he said. "He came and told me, and you know what? There *are* horses in heaven. Jesus rides on a big white one."

Consider starting a short term support group for grieving pet owners, (especially kids). Walk through the process step by step as I suggest in chapter two. Here are some helpful things to ask someone who has lost a pet. "How many years was it that Sabrina was part of your family? Did she bond with one member of the family more than with others?" "Tell me about Fido's personality. She always seemed so good natured." "Do you remember a time when Woofie did something really special?" "What's your fondest memory of Sedgley?" "You mentioned that Teddy always brought you the paper every morning. I'll bet you're having a tough time adjusting to the change in your routine." "Tell me about Tadbury's battle with diabetes. Did her personality change as the disease progressed? When did you realize something wasn't quite right?" "What do you miss the most now that Kolby has died?" "Did your kids get to say goodbye to Freckles before she died? **Are there things you wish you could have said to her that you didn't get a chance to say? In your mind's eye, picture her here in front of you, and say what you need to say to her, now.**" "Where are you going to place her body?" (Cremated remains) "Is your family planning to get together soon to remember Kongo and talk about him?"

**Honey The Rock Hound:** Everyone at camp laughed hilariously as they watched my cocker spaniel puppy leap repeatedly into the air. Each time her feet left the ground her long curly ears flapped out to the sides giving the appearance she was trying to fly. Actually she was straining to see where the rocks landed that my grandchildren were chucking in the woods for her. She'd grovel in the underbrush, searching for long periods of time, half yipping and half growling. Invariably, she'd return and spit the same rock at the feet of whoever had thrown it.

As time went on, small rocks began turning up inside the house, under the furniture. The pup was hiding them in her mouth when she came in. Later when no one was looking, she'd drag them out and roll on them to scratch her back. Thus we dubbed her "Honey The Rock Hound."

Recently I wrote a kid's book about her. In the story she runs under a truck and is killed. In a subtle way the story takes kids step by step through the grieving process. It grapples with tough issues others often avoid, like "I'm mad at God! Why didn't God answer **MY** prayer? Will I see my puppy that died, in heaven? How can my pet be buried out back under the lilac tree and be in heaven with God at the same time?"

Kids feel pain and loss. In the book, Joey, Honey's master, experiences anxiety, as he wonders if it's his puppy that was run over by a truck. He turns to God in prayer and tastes disappointment and despair when his prayer is not answered. Joey sensed what it's like to be in a daze, bewildered and not able to function normally in his everyday activities. He feels the anger and frustration of having to talk about his loss with someone he doesn't particularly like. Joey was able to say the things he needed to say to his pet, later that evening, when he spent time alone with the little dog's body.

Joey and his family felt loved and supported as neighbors came together at the time of the accident, and again for the time of remembrance. Joey's extended family comes together to share memories and love. Photos and special items like her collar and leash, a favorite toy, a well chewed slipper and one of her rocks was displayed, to help everyone remember Honey, as they knew her. Everyone was reminded that God loves all creatures, just as He loves them and that there is hope beyond the grave.

Later, Joey and his folks have a long discussion about whether or not to get another puppy right away, to take their minds off Honey. The decision to let the grieving process take its course first, is decided on and Joey is made to understand that latent emotions like anger and frustration can be taken out on a new pet, without understanding why.

Once a child identifies with Joey, and accepts the process of working through his or her grief as it is shown in the book, they will be empowered to help anyone facing death or loss. I'd like to think the grief recovery principles will stay with them for life. Call it "A Crash Course In Grief Recovery For Kids." There's *not* a whole lot of difference for a young child, dealing with the loss of a beloved pet or the death of a loved one. The book can be a powerful teaching tool for parents, home schoolers or others reading it to a child. It gives anyone an opportunity to express their own grief, present or delayed, and it encourages extended family and neighbors to share in one another's grief.

The book, Honey the Rock Hound (A Crash Course in Grief Recovery for Kids) is best suited for children 8 to 14, or for anyone that has recently experienced the death of a pet. It may be ordered on line from **www.trafford.com #06-297**

I wonder if Christ had a little black dog
All curly and wooly like mine
With two shiny eyes and a nose round and wet
And eyes brown and tender that shine.
I'm sure if he had that the little black dog
Knew right from the start He was God!
That he needed no proof that Christ was Divine,
But just worshipped the ground where He trod
I'm afraid that He didn't, because I have read
How He prayed in the garden alone,
When all of his friends and disciples had fled
Even Peter, the one called a stone.
And oh I am sure a little black dog
With a heart so t ender and warm,
Would never have left Him to suffer alone,
But creeping right under His arm
would have licked those dear fingers in agony clasped
And counting all favors as lost,
When they took Him away, would have trotted behind
And followed Him right to the cross.

**Elizabeth Gardiner Reynolds**

A child should be encouraged to express his or her emotions in an acceptable way. Excessive crying, hugging and moments of anger or sadness should be talked about with the child. Grief should not be suppressed, but if these actions become excessive, and you'll know instinctively if they are, help should be sought. Grieving children sometimes feel responsible for situations they have no control over, like rejection or abuse, They don't understand divorce and of course not death. Be on the lookout for anger, withdrawal (or worse). Encourage role-playing, drawing, coloring and talking about the deceased pet or loved one by name, *often*.

Some people will tell a child that when someone dies they have "gone to sleep". if they do, they are apt to find themselves, as one family did, with a child who is terrified of going to sleep. I went to a home once, to make arrangements for an infant's burial. There was a little two or three year old girl there that was just having an awful time. I mentioned it to the mother and she said, "She's mad at me, because someone told her I had gone to the hospital and 'lost' the baby."

**Kids ask some tough questions.** Here are some acceptable answers. For example, a child may say, "My Sunday School teacher says everyone is *not* going to heaven, but you say ***all*** the animals will be there, who's right?" One way to answer is. "We can't play ball on both the Red Sox and Yankees ball team at the same time. Neither can we be on God's team and the devil's. We have to make a choice of who's team we want to be on and since God knows what we are thinking (Psalm **139),** He knows who's team we are really on. God isn't going to let anyone from the devil's team into heaven. God has given humans the ability to know the difference between right and wrong, good and evil, going back to Adam and Eve. Animals don't have that ability. All their spirits go to be with God when they die. The Bible tells us God knows when even a sparrow falls. A child may ask how a pet can be buried out back under the lilac bush (or in the woods) and be with God at the same time. The Honey book uses the illustration of an astronaut. They can't live in space, without a space suit. Our body is our space suit while we're here on earth. It can't move unless our spirit directs it to.

For young children: Drawing or coloring a picture which in some way expresses their feelings; something they have done with the one they are grieving for, or something they remember them (or their pet) doing. Placing the picture in the casket, under a sod at the grave or leaving it with an adult also helps. A letter or a tape recording for an older child is very helpful, too. For example: "Dear aunt Lil, here are some things I didn't get a chance to say to you before. You really were my favorite aunt, etc". Have them share it with others close to them. If it's possible have them place it in the casket with the deceased loved one. Placing something meaningful with the loved one is also helpful. The family didn't ask my opinion, but someone euthanized a pet cat and placed it's body with a young woman that died.

I've seen it dozens of times. A pet dies and the owners rush right out and get another pet. They may exchange a dog for a kitten, but they really don't take the time they need to grieve the death of the animal they had. They try to drown their sorrow in something to take up their mind and the loneliness they feel. All of the "stages of grief" we looked at in chapter two; have to be worked through when a pet dies, just as it does with the death of a loved one. If there is still anger, a person, especially a child, may abuse the new pet, or verbally snap at people. Don't think you are doing someone a favor by getting them a new puppy or kitten. Someone did that for us shortly after our Honey died. It was a very difficult adjustment for the new puppy. He just didn't "fit" and eventually had to be returned, causing hurt feelings and disappointment all around.

A word about children and visiting hours at a funeral home. If a parent, grandparent or other loved one has died, I suggest you take the child to the funeral home before, or between, visiting hours. He or she needs to see the flowers and their loved one in the casket. They need to grieve, ask questions and be shown love. With so many scary things on TV etc. today, they need to know the truth. They also need to be allowed to take part in the grieving process with the rest of the family.

## Divorced & Singles Group

"I almost think I'd rather be a widow," my friend confided in me. She was a lovely middle aged woman with four great kids. Her husband had left her for another woman. She expressed her pain eloquently. It seems to me that it is much harder to get over (or through) a divorce than a death. With the death of a spouse, family and community come together to express love and support for the one(s) left behind. There's closure; usually with some kind of service, where people can vent their emotions. Divorce or separation is something like a worm in an apple. You never know when, or where the other person can poke his or her head out. There's no closure, just constant anxiety and pain. Relationships that have formed over the years with the other person's family, are, at best on shaky ground. No one knows exactly what to say so they don't say anything, and withdraw. Financial hardships often result, so that factor becomes an embarrassment.

It's very painful when people have to put on a mask and attend family functions with the former mate there. We live in a couple-oriented society. Friends are reluctant to invite the single person to social events, because there is secret anxiety that the single person will make a "play" for someone's spouse.

With a divorce, or separation, the grieving person portrays the other person as a villain. In your grief recovery groups, try to get the grieving party to remember some good times he or she shared with the other person. There must have been something about them that they loved enough to have had a relationship. Remember, forgiveness *must* occur before healing will begin. In most cases, *both* people grieve when a relationship falls apart. Be alert to delayed grief, months, or even years later.

**Don't even *have* a divorced or singles "*group*".** Invite only one or two people going through a divorce or separation into your grief recovery groups, rather than having a group of divorced or separated people. Later if someone wants to tell a friend about how you helped them, invite that person to your next group, or start with that one person, forming a new mixed group, (mixed grieving *situations*, not men and women). Don't make a production out of mending fractured relationships.

**Don't even hint of doing any counseling or therapy. YOU ARE NOT a therapist.** You're helping a friend (or someone you know), over the biggest hurdle in their lives. You are giving them a chance to vent and express themselves, in an acceptable way. The person suffering the loss of a relationship is grieving just as much as the person experiencing the death of a spouse or child. You are safe to put someone grieving the death of a mate in a group with someone grieving a fractured marriage or relationship. **THIS TYPE OF SUPPORT GROUP IS BEST CONDUCTED IN A CHURCH SETTING. See the section on church support groups in chapter four.**

## Sailing In Uncharted Waters

**Stillborn Children: There's** a real need out there for committed people to work with parents (especially the mothers) of stillborn children. There's much more bonding of a pregnant woman and her unborn child than most of us realize. When the child dies, even after only a few months of pregnancy, *serious* grieving takes place! (Refer to chapter one.) Only the parents, often only the mother, understand the deep emotional wounds that occur. Even close family is most often unaware of the grief.

Definitely separate mothers who have miscarried during early pregnancy, and parents who have lost children during late term pregnancy. In any situation, encourage the parent(s) to include their close relatives and friends. It's best to work with *just one family at a time.*

Families that have had services (with close friends and extended family present) for stillborn or premature babies have gone on and healed well. Encourage the parents to name the child if they have not already done so. To have a place they can go to, like a family lot in the cemetery, or a little shrine in the home, or flower garden, where they can place flowers and grieve.

The death of a child at birth is often downplayed. That mother especially needs closure. The father, too, but not as much, perhaps. I was convinced of this when a young mother who had grown up next door to our funeral home experienced the premature death of her first born. I took the child to her home, and experienced a family in mourning. By the time the service was over, I understood how important it was for that family to come together and grieve.

I suggest you do everything as you would for any other support group. The child is **_real_**. The mother (and very possibly the father) has bonded with the child, much more than we realize or appreciate. You have the tools you need to begin an outreach program. Talk to psychotherapists, maternity center staff, OBGYN clinics, Right to Life agencies, maternity wards at hospitals, homes for unwed mothers, adoption agencies, nurses, funeral homes and professional people. Remember, you are not offering counseling or therapy, **just a *support* group that gets positive results.**

More and more hospitals today are encouraging mothers (and fathers) to hold their stillborn babies following their birth; this offers a family closure with the child and a way to say good-bye.

The first time I experienced a family wanting to hold a deceased child was when a toddler accidentally drowned. The family (grandparents too) spent hours just holding the child and expressing their grief and love for it.

**Miscarriages:** Most of us have not given the attention we should to the bonding of a mother and her unborn child, especially during the early stages of pregnancy. In many instances severe emotional strain results following miscarriage. The mother will often need counseling. Dads should be made aware that closure needs to take place, for him as well as the mother. A gathering of family and close friends to share the hopes and dreams the parents had for the little one is very important. "You can always have more kids" just doesn't cut it! I know women who have stayed in bed weeks trying to keep from miscarrying, because they wanted the child so badly.

Feelings should be shared. The parents are both hurting, especially the mom. The loss is real. We tend to think that just because the child has not been carried to full term, it somehow isn't a "real" child.

It won't be hard to get a few women together that have experienced miscarriage and start a support group (just word of mouth). There's more later in the book on ways to facilitate a meaningful groups.

You have all that you need to begin an outreach to parents. Talk to staff at maternity centers, OBGYN clinics, to Life agencies, maternity wards at hospitals, homes for unmarried mothers, adoption agencies, nurses and professional people. You are better to start with someone you know. They will know others. Go from there.

## Section Four

# Empowering People

The "support group" concept has been used effectively for good as well as evil for many years. The Communists called them "cell groups" and succeeded in infiltrating and subverting many governments, including our own. The largest Christian church in the world, in South Korea, operates very effectively with home churches, using the small group concept. The medical profession has effectively used support groups to encourage people suffering from almost every kind of malady there is.

After WWII a guy named Deming tried to get the American auto industry to adapt the "team" approach to manufacturing. His idea was simple. Get *everybody in the* workplace involved with *every*thing; in every aspect of what's being made. Nobody in Detroit would listen to him, so he took his idea to the Japanese. The result was, as you know, their autos and electronics dominated world markets for years. I witnessed a glaring example of workplace stubbornness, and a classic example of what I'm talking about. A neighbor of mine, a floor sweeper at a paper company, figured out how to solve a problem with the conveyer system. It had frustrated engineers for years. But in spite of his willingness to help, the experts would not even listen to my neighbor's suggestions!

## 101 Battle Tested P/R Strategies for Successful Funeral Directors

It's taken over 60 years, but today, most business and industry in America has, at least in part, adopted Deming's principles of teamwork, even though they may not have given him credit for perfecting it. To refresh your memory, here they are: Be consistent. Be sure everyone is working toward defined long term goals. Break down barriers to good communications. Adopt new philosophies. Eliminate mistakes altogether. Study and define. Cease mass inspections. Buy the best quality—it saves time and money in the long run. Constantly improve services, systems and production.

Get everyone involved in every aspect of the operation. Constantly train and retrain workers. Show them how to do their job beter (mentoring). Make work easier. Eliminate everything that impedes production. Make it OK to point out problems. Listen to suggestions for solving them. Eliminate empty slogans. They're irritating and meaningless.

I would add another one. Reward employees for new ideas and cost saving techniques. I would also include rewards excellence, positive attitude, and commitment to the organization's overall goals. Deming proved that industry could produce superior products by getting e*veryone,* including the floor sweeper, involved in every aspect of the operation. Any manager will tell you, that many issues in the workplace are the result of someone bringing a gut wrenching, personal problem to work with them. (It's *very difficult* not to!) Many people in leadership roles do not understand that the real "root" of many of these problems is grief.

Everything a person does, is affected by their grief. It also affects everyone else around them. They will likely have difficulty staying focused on anything. If you ask them to do something they'll very likely say, "yes", but what you have said just does *not register!* People who are grieving intensely, often have difficulty performing routine tasks. They'll probably be unable to interact normally with co-workers, and they'll likely be oblivious to safety hazards around them. If they work around machinery, or heavy equipment, or if they are required to make critical decisions on the job, someone needs to ask them to take a few days off!

No one is immune from grief. We're all vulnerable. It can affect our attitude with co-workers, production, and even indirectly, customer satisfaction.

More than 50% of an average manager's time is spent trying to correct someone's "goof". The number of top managers who buckle under from stress each year is staggering. I believe much of that pressure could be relieved if support groups were functioning at the employee level.

By combining grief recovery principles as outlined in the book, with Deming's concept of the team approach, you can transform your workplace, your church, and whatever other organizations you may be affiliated with, for good. When teaching anyone to read a map, and follow a compass, the first thing they must learn is how to *"orient"* their compass from *magnetic north* to *"true" north* on the map. If they don't understand that, they'll almost certainly miss their destination, if they travel very far. If only managers and team leaders would *orient their thinking* a few degrees, and recognize that *grief recovery, like magnetic north,* can be the determining factor of where anyone ends up after a crisis in their lives.

There are probably many reasons why grief recovery support groups are not practical for your particular work situation: you're too busy, it's too complicated, it might not work, nobody's interested, it's never been done before, on and on." There is, however, one very good reason why the new grief recovery concept just might work for you. It's called **"contentment"**.

"I was so proud of my dad," my friend told me. "He was a dairyman, and he had a herd *of 'contented' cows!'* I thought, "how great it would be, if everyone in the *workplace* could be as *contented* as those cows." Your in-house support group can *go a long way* toward assuring that *everyone* on *your team* **is** *"contented"*.

With over forty years in funeral service, I'd like to share a few suggestions to help you keep the people in your workplace a little more contented.

The first and most important suggestion would be to *improve communication skills.* Small group facilitators could do a lot more to assure that everyone in the workplace is informed about daily activities and policy decisions. I can't place my finger on the statistics, but most people who are fired from job were let go *because they did not understand what was expected of them!* That comfirms the sad fact that a very small percent of businesses of any kind, offer training or mentoring for their employees. So mentoring would have to be very near the top of the contentment barometer. As more employees become facilitators, they will adopt the helpful hints for communicating effectively, and managing group dynamics.

If someone does a job well, praise them publicly, ASAP. Let others know about it. If it's unique or special, be sure and do something nice for them; possibly a bonus. This will go a long way toward making sure your high achiever stays contented. High achievers thrive on praise and they strive for *excellence.* You'll be blessed by the employee that would rather train someone for a particular skill and see them get credit for mastering it, than seizing the limelight themselves. Cherish that person.

Be on the lookout for the person who kind of blends in with other employees. They work hard, but they'd rather work within a group. By and large these people are *not interested* in being a star performer. They're more contented when *everyone* in their group is getting the credit.

A very important ingredient in the contentment mix would be a revision of the company policy statement *by your employees* themselves. You'd be encouraging camaraderie, understanding, and communications between everyone, and they will feel like they have ownership in your organization.

Never criticize anyone where others will see or hear you. Be specific in telling that person what was wrong, and how it affected the organization. Communicate that it is the person's particular *action* that you are talking about, not his or her overall performance. When you are finished, shake hands with the person so they know you still appreciate them. Communicate that the issue is over with, and that's the end of it. If the problem is serious, get a trusted employee or someone with more authority than you have, to be a witness. Have the person sign a document stating what happened, and everything that was discussed. Be very careful not to place yourself in a compromising situation if the person being reprimanded is of the opposite sex.

I firmly believe, that the more every employee knows about the intricacies of the organization and all it's operations, the stronger the organization becomes.

Multi-tasking always appealed to me. No organization should have to depend on just one person for any function.

When *we* are in any kind of trouble and someone extends a helping hand, we instinctively want to return the favor. If it's an employee who's been freed from that awful load of grief they've been carrying around, for God only knows how long, they *can't help but appreciate it*! If the (grief recovery support group) program is sponsored by the organization they are affiliated with, like a church, police, or fire department, veterans group, etc. the person who has been freed *will almost certainly* reward that organization with increased loyalty and dedication.

Every business and organization has specific characteristics that make it unique. The personalities of leadership certainly set the agenda. I am assuming that every manager is striving for excellence in their particular field. My goal is to point out the areas where I feel support groups would help the staff be more contented and the clients more at home and comfortable. Management, as well as employees, have needs that can be addressed more effectively in a support group setting.

This chapter is intended to show you how to apply the information we talked about earlier in the book, to your workplace, your church, or any other group or organization in which you may be involved. I'd like for you to make a critical assessment of your personal situation, and if it's feasible, to organize a support group, using the guidelines in chapter 6. See if grief could be an underlying factor with any of the problems you encounter in your work or other activities. There may not be pressing problems at the moment, but I suggest you prepare for the gut-wrenching situation any one of us could find ourselves in, at any time. Anyway, I hope this book has helped you recognize whether or not a person needs professional counseling or therapy. If there is any doubt in your mind, err on the assumption that they do.

## To Nursing Home & Extended Care Facility

**Oooooh**, for just five minutes of tranquility! How many times a day do you wish you could just get that awful load of *grief* off your back, kick off your shoes, and enjoy five minutes of tranquility? Of all the places in the world for a health care professional to work, the nursing home must be the most depressing! Every time you turn around you're dealing with grief. You can't get away from it! *Every family* comes to you *grieving*, and the patient is *grieving WORSE*. Your staff not only has to deal with the dying patient, but *their intensely grieving family members* too. When the patient dies, your staff has to continue to work *with* your patient's family, and *the other patients who* had day to day contact with the deceased patient. In many cases, there is bonding with other staff and the patient, as well as cleaning staff, physical therapists, activities directors, hair dressers, volunteers, and others.

Brace yourself: here's some *good* news, a psychological shot in the arm! Introducing a *comprehensive* grief recovery program for your nursing home that will (hopefully), **uplift everyone's spirits, put a *sparkle* in their eyes, a *smile* on their faces, a *spring* in their step and a renewed *zest for life*.** It will eliminate 90% of *your* stress (well, almost) cause your P/R to sky rocket, empower you and your people to help hurting families, and make your facility a household word in your community. It will also help you maintain your own sanity.

I recently invited a friend of mine, who was having a difficult time admitting her mother to an extended care facility, to sit in on a support group at our church. Her comment hit me like a bolt of lightning and completely changed my attitude about grief recovery support groups for all time. "What I *really* wish you'd do," she exclaimed, "is to start a support group for people who have to place their loved ones in a nursing home!"

Those words flung open the door to a vast expanse of virgin territory, an area of opportunity and service, waiting for anyone willing to step through and claim it. It's a brand new concept: **Facilitating grief recovery support groups for grieving families *before* their loved one dies.**

From the time a family realizes their loved one really is going to die, and needs professional care, they are usually overwhelmed with grief and all it's ugly facets. At the same time, they have to try and figure out how to deal with their loved one's complex personal issues, towering like a mountain over them. Some of these things require immediate attention. It's no wonder they are overwhelmed as they jump through the hoops, trying to get their loved one admitted to a nursing home. There is so much confusion, so much stress, and so much grief; particularly grief, the relatives have to endure, and the only thing most of them know to do is *"stuff it"*. Actually you are holding the key to grief recovery in your hands, right now.

Any social worker that is familiar with grief recovery material will be able to adapt and use mature volunteers as facilitators for these groups. Just loan them this book. At least, families trying to admit their loved one to a nursing home, have social workers to turn to. Unfortunately, many families in your community at large, do not have a nursing home social worker to turn to. The possibility of reaching out beyond your walls, to the public at large, seems to me to be the ultimate P/R opportunity.

Once your social workers read this material they will have a greater appreciation of the emotional turmoil families of patients are suffering through. Use the guidelines as a way to help someone get what's bothering them off their chest. The same guidelines apply, when working with small grief recovery support groups, or for a person in crisis. Just having someone to talk with is a blessing.

There's a heavy load of grief weighing down your patients' families. Support groups can help them get rid of it.

I suggest you begin the process when a family *first* inquires about admitting their loved one to your facility. Whether or not the patient is admitted, invite that family to sit in on a support group. The P/R advantages for your nursing home far outweigh the extra time your facilitator will need to spend with that family. I don't have to mention it to you, but it might be weeks, or even months, before that patient is admitted anywhere. In the meantime, you have helped that family get over their worst hurdle: the initial stages of grief, shock, disbelief, bewilderment, anger, etc.

Everyone needs closure; a way to say goodbye and a way to express their FEELINGS in an acceptable manner (preferably *to* their loved one before they die).

Recently a friend of mine who worked nights in a state hospital told about sitting with dying patients. She said many would die around 2 AM, and by 7 AM there would be no trace that the patient had ever been there. The personal effects had been bagged; the body cleaned up, placed in a shroud, and moved out. The records were in the Administrator's office, and life went on as usual. Well, not quite. *Everyone was grieving by themselves and there was no acceptable way to express it.*

There was no closure for the staff that had bonded with the patient; no way to express their feelings of grief, relief, or whatever. There was no way for the other patients to express *their* feelings either. The attitude was cold and seemingly uncaring. We often overlook the bonding that takes place between a caregiver and a patient. There has to be some, especially if the patient has been with you for any length of time. The bonds that sometimes develop between patients and other patients' families can sometimes be strong. As hard as your staff may try *not* to let it happen, relationships are formed between family of patients and staff. It's also easy to over-look relationships between the patients themselves.

When my mother was in a nursing home, I remember one feisty lady in a wheel-chair who would really work hard the days she could, straining to get from another wing in the facility to my mother's room, just to chat with her for a few minutes.

On days she could not make it, no one dropped in to tell my mother why. When she died, it was several days before my mother found out. No one let her know how her friend was doing, during her last days, and THERE WAS NO CLOSURE—no way for two friends to say good-bye. There was no closure between the staff and the patient and probably none between staff and family. How much better it would have been if my mother and some of the other patients, with the staff, had come together for just a few minutes, reflected on some of the unique things about this woman and <u>SAID</u> what they didn't get a chance to *say to her*. If everyone was involved, cleaning staff included, this type of thing would not happen.

A grieving person <u>does</u> affect everyone around them. Years ago I persuaded a nursing home owner to let me do a grief recovery workshop for his staff. At the end of the day we asked if anyone had grief issues they wanted us to help resolve. Several in the room immediately pointed to one man and said, almost in unison, _____does!"_____had lost his wife and family in a terrible accident several years before. It had affected the attitude of everyone that worked with him. Undoubtedly it had affected his productivity too. When he walked out of the room that day, he was like a new person. He had been able to say his goodbyes to his family and complete his relationship with them. Everyone in the room that day was upbeat too. A support group would have saved him from carrying his load of grief around all those years. Undoubtedly, efficiency and attitude would have improved.

When one of my mother's nursing home cleaning ladies left, all my mother could say was, "I don't think she's here anymore." It was ever so small, but there was a bond that developed between the two of them. If it's not appropriate for staff to make the rounds before leaving for another job or on retirement, have some specific communication so patients (who can understand), and their families, know what's happening.

After activities, or meals, when patients are gathered together anyway, everyone could take a few moments and remember that person. I know everyone's busy. I know the urgency to get the necessities over with, but somewhere, somehow, there needs to be a few minutes when staff, friends and family of a deceased patient can come together just to say good-bye! Like steam in a tea kettle, emotions need to be let out! Patients have lots of time to think. This will give them something to think about and occupy a few more minutes of their day. It will seem a little more like home, when they know what's happening to people they come in contact with often. We complain about old folks being "nosey", but that's their world. Keeping informed gives them a reason to get out of bed every morning.

To give the family of a patient that has died, the opportunity to express their feelings, publicly, to say good-bye to everyone that's been so nice to them while their loved one was at your facility, would be very therapeutic and a great morale booster for everyone(great P/R too). I'll bet a nickel that everyone on your staff would step a little livelier, be more apt to have a smile on their faces, try a little harder and take on a whole new zest for life, if they knew they were appreciated, and probably going to be publicly recognized by the patient's families for their extra effort. They MIGHT just try a little harder to please difficult patients, and go the extra mile.

Invite your volunteers to take part in the grief recovery process too. I'll bet you'll see an increase in day to day enthusiasm, as well as an increase in the numbers of volunteers.

Let me make a suggestion. Purchase a couple of these books and loan them to your staff and volunteers. The better EVERYONE understands the grief recovery process the more they can contribute to each patient's well being and the well being of everyone else. The time they spend talking with patients and encouraging them, is as crucial to the patient's progress as any medication. With management's commitment to take grief recovery seriously, you should soon see a gradual attitude change in your patients and staff alike. The extra time your people spend helping patients through the grief recovery process will be more than made up for by their increased efficiency, positive mental attitude and commitment(not only to your organization, but more so to their own support group!) Group dynamics are powerful! People want to take part in what's going on, to make a significant contribution to the well being of the organization. Giving them the tools to contribute to each patient's overall recovery(in this case grief recovery)will allow them to constantly see positive results.

I REALIZE THIS MAY REQUIRE SOME MODIFICATION OF WORK RULES, BUT ISN'T YOUR ULTIMATE GOAL THE WELL BEING AND CONTENTMENT OF EACH PATIENT? NEW REGULATIONS AND RESTRICTIONS IMPOSED ON YOU MAY ALTER EVERYTHING. I SINCERELY EMPATHIZE WITH YOU!

Did you ever consider having your own grief recovery support groups for families of deceased patients? It's a golden P/R opportunity. Once your volunteer facilitators become familiar with the program it pretty much runs itself. Everything is spelled out step by step. All it takes is the desire to help hurting people over the biggest bump in their road of life. New facilitators are gleaned from groups that have completed their recovery. Actually most anyone can take this book, use it as a guide, and facilitate a recovery group cold turkey. However don't expect someone recently widowed or who has gone through some type of calamity in the few months to be *emotionally ready* to do it.

Any social worker would be more than qualified, but probably would not want to make the time commitment or become emotionally involved enough to facilitate a group long term (Chapter two). A woman who has been widowed more than a year *would probably* be a great choice to facilitate a grief recovery support group. Your sense of how well she has worked through the grieving process herself will be your determining factor.

Here's another radical idea. Have support groups each day, or several times a week for patients that are able to communicate with each other. Get your volunteers involved in facilitating these groups. Contented patients live longer and everyone around them is happier! Involving your volunteers in the grief recovery process, will help new patients work through their grief issues sooner. Put one of these books in your volunteer's hands and test me on this one.

Here's a suggestion. It will take a little more time, jockeying patients around at first, but pairing them together as roommates with other patients that they can communicate with *on their own level* would, in some cases, lead to an improvement in their positive mental attitude. Again, how do you spell contentment?

*Loan* a copy of this book to anyone and everyone that has contact with your patients: beauticians first, then housekeeping, PT people, food service, and even maintenance people. Get as many people involved as possible! There's a lot of grief out there that doesn't have to be! **I have no idea what the nursing home of the future will look like, but we can all dream of the ideal situation. God Bless You**

This could help make a life appreciation or memorial type of service more meaningful. The service actually begins when the patient arrives at your facility. Someone snaps a photo of him or her on their arrival, or soon afterwards. A few notes are taken by a volunteer who just happens to stop by to say hello and help the new patient settle in. At that time a special folder is opened on the patient. It follows them wherever they go in the facility. Who is he friendly with? Who are the friends that visited her often? What were his hobbies? What were her likes and dislikes? Did someone remember his birthday? What activities did she take part in? Everyone at the nursing home gets involved. Casual conversation keeps everyone updated. They are like a big family. Even the hairdresser takes part.

Each one of the staff adds an occasional note to the folder and snaps some candid photos. It wouldn't take a volunteer very long to put together a brief compilation of these notes and photos from time to time. These could be shared at his or her life appreciation service and then given to the patient's family. PS: It would be a great P/R tool. Share it with the family during your periodic assessment time with them. After the patient' death, the folder could be used to put together a meaningful life appreciation presentation and then given to the family as a keepsake. In your next newsletter, and on your next printed letterhead, add the words, "We treat *everyone* like our own family." Ask your staff to adopt it as a motto, and live by it!

The following may not be possible because of security, confidentiality, etc. I call it "The scrapbook project." Have a nice scrapbook in your lobby or activities room, with a photo and a brief blip about each patient (not just a mug shot.) If you have a large facility, place a scrapbook at the entrance of each day room, or in the various lounges. It would let visitors know who their loved one's neighbors are. (Privacy laws may prohibit this so maybe photos with just the patient's first name?) Something similar could be kept and shared at the patient's life appreciation service, when the time comes.

This project is perfect for teenage volunteers to get involved with. You might even offer one page in it for each family to decorate in honor of their loved one. Volunteers could be assigned to help decorate the pages. It would be a tribute to each patient's life. I am sure others will appreciate knowing what the person did before becoming your patient. If the patient's families can't do it, your teenage volunteers, or different groups, like church ladies, or support groups would welcome the opportunity to get involved and be creative.

Teenage volunteers have a lot of potential. Your board of directors will have to decide whether of not to keep the scrapbook and share it with the public, years down the line.

In time this could become priceless, as future generations research their roots. If you start this, be sure and laminate and add the person's obit when the time comes. You might want to remove each patient's page when he or she dies, and present it to the patient's family.

If the patient has a photo on record, it could be used on a little remembrance paper and passed out as a keepsake at their memorial service. Have a few extra for staff who couldn't be there and extras for family to send to relatives and friends from away. Offer to make extra copies for them at your cost. Include one in your next newsletter. Visitors that became acquainted with the patient, but do not know their name, might get the news letter and not have seen the obituary, or they may have known the patient by sight only. Place a copy in the scrapbook as a memorial, and let it be known that copies are available. If you do not have a newsletter and want to compose one, get in touch with me.

If older kids volunteer, assign each one a couple of specific patients to spend time with when they visit. That way there's continuity, and bonding, a bit more like home. Ask the volunteer to read this book. They could do a lot to help the patient deal with their personal grief issues.

Why not have a brief memorial type service for patients and staff, following the death of a long term patient, or loss of a staff person? Pause and bring patients and staff together, perhaps right after the evening meal.) Even better, wait a few days and invite the patient's family too. Plan a time of remembrance between shifts, or at a convenient time for BOTH shifts. (You could even have *two* services). Once your staff understands the importance of the grieving process, they will try to make things easier and better for everyone. The workplace will become more like a family, because everyone will communicate better. The staff will be better appreciated by the patients, and *more so* by the patient's families. **Workers will have a greater sense of personal satisfaction and take greater pride in their tasks.**

Suggestion: have a memorial service for all the (long term) patients that have died during the past month. Include families and staff that can make it. If it was scheduled between work shifts, could more staff attend? Those that could not, would be encouraged to express their feelings at their weekly support groups.

## Owners, Managers, H R Professionals

Your life will be so much easier with grief recovery support groups! Paul Harvey used to say that when there's a problem, and people sit down and talk about it, "all the steam blows off in the whistle". He's referring to the old time steam engine on a freight train.

What's the best way to set up support groups in a large organization? I would just refer back to what Deming was able to accomplish in Japan. If you have support groups it will certainly lead to better understanding. However, everyone there has to be willing to be candid with each other, and have a sincere desire to help one another and see the company prosper. The most important thing as I see it is for leaders of existing teams, pods or whatever they are called in your organization, to become familiar with the grief recovery process, and work it into the team meetings when someone brings a personal problem to work with them. There very well may be work-related situations where people are grieving, such as possible loss of a co-worker, lay-offs, or retirement of co-workers, or serious illness of a fellow employee.

I can't stress enough: if there is a serious situation, personal or work related, the best thing to do is deal with it ASAP. Other people's safety may be involved. Certainly everyone's attitude will be affected. Production and efficiency will be affected. My experience with groups is, that once everyone understands the nature of the problem, they will all rally around the one suffering and pick up the slack. Being aware of the problem, will motivate others to be more alert to what's going on.

If you operate in a hostile environment, support groups probably won't work. If people can forget differences, come together and pitch in, everyone benefits. Understanding the grieving process will definitely help everyone deal with the nitty-gritty issues. Even if you start with just one small group in your own department and build on that, it should grow. Later on you may be in a position to put the principles to work in a different environment. If nothing else, you will be better equipped to handle crisis in your own life, your family's, your friends' and co-workers'.

Politics will have to determine if a supervisor should be a group facilitator. I do believe that groups could be set up around general work areas. People that interact well with each other in day to day activities could be placed in groups.

Try this: Hand pick people you know who would make good facilitators. Then decide who you would like to work with. Loan them this book and ask them to read it with the idea they might like to work with you facilitating your first group. It's a slow process.

If you begin your own group, don't forget to include the floor sweeper, and a cross section of workers in every group. Remember the conveyer story, and my neighbor. Work with your original group for several months, until everyone is familiar with group dynamics, and have had an opportunity to unload any grief issues they might be carrying around with them. Then ask each of them to go out and put together their own group. Four other people max plus their own assistant facilitator (who has or will read the book.) There should be a minimum of two others plus an assistant facilitator to start a group. From each of those new groups, one person should eventually be selected to read the book, and consider becoming an assistant at some future date. This way you have someone from your leadership team and an assistant facilitator. The process of picking an assistant facilitator repeats itself.

Within a year or so, everyone in your organization should be in a support group, with the leadership (facilitator) of each group familiar with the grief recovery process. Someone else is asked to read the book, and invited to become an assistant facilitator when the group splits next time. Don't hurry the process of raising up new facilitators. Be sure they have enough experience and actually want to assume leadership of a new group. Also be sure a person has adequately worked through their own grief issues before trying to help others.

At some point everyone in the organization is a member of a group. Only when new employees join the company do the groups expand and split. Strong bonds develop. I feel confident you will see amazing things happen, at some point in the process *each time* you facilitate a group.

Invite the facilitators to a monthly leadership meeting for a discussion. There is always a seasoned facilitator and an assistant. The senior facilitator will now begin the process again, mentoring a new assistant. Your original leadership team members have now become individual mentors for new facilitators, as they continue to lead their own groups with assistant facilitators training under them.

You will have to use your own feelings about when to split the groups and strike off with a new lead facilitator. After your first group, try and be sure a seasoned facilitator and an assistant, who has read the book, team up to facilitate each group. Your ultimate goal is to establish long-lasting groups which really get to know each other and work well together as a team. Let them pick their own best time for weekly meetings. People who didn't quite fit in a group may well become very active and involved once everyone decides to be courteous and understanding. We all need to learn to overlook a person's quirks and respect them for who they are. I've found *we all have* unlovely quirks. Ours are just different from other people's. Learn to over-look them, and respect the person for who they are, not what they might say or do. This could take a few weeks. Be courteous. Remember the old saying, "Your actions speak so loud they can't hear what you are saying."

Keep groups below eight. Once someone has read the book and gone through several months with a group, they'll have enough skills to sit in as a facilitator in a new group. I think it's important for facilitators to get together once a month and talk over problems and strategy. In addition to reviewing the grief recovery process it will be wise to review Deming's principles too.

I'll say it again. It's almost impossible to leave a serious personal problem at home. *It takes someone with a serious grief issue at least three times as long as usual to process anything.* So if it's not possible for the person to go home, insist that someone monitor them closely. Follow up on all of their decisions, and insist they do not operate machinery or heavy equipment.

By recognizing that a problem may be grief-related you've gone a long way to solving it. I can't tell you how important it is for someone in a crisis to have other people who care take the time and listen to them, to help them sort things out in their mind. Assemble the person's grief recovery support group ASAP, and even if it means that they slack off on the job for a while, they'll more than make it up later! (And so will everyone else in the support group.) Obviously I can't guarantee that, but if for no other reason, a person in grief may be a hazard to himself or herself, and affect the attitude of everyone around them.

## Funeral Service Professional

Is funeral service going the way of the buggy whip? Can it stay afloat in these economically troubled waters, or will it go under like the Titanic? Funeral directors have always done well under pressure and adapted to change. Following the Civil War it was *embalming*. In the 30's, *funeral homes* were introduced. My grandfather, a store-front undertaker, nearly went out of business when a new guy in town opened one in competition with him. Following WW II, *cement vaults* became readily available. Cremation has grown from a tiny fraction of our business to perhaps the most significant factor ahead. There was near panic when *the FTC slapped their "rules"* on the industry—but we survived and thrived. Many of us panicked when the *giant conglomerates* arrived. We have all had to learn about *computers and the internet*. Is there anyone that does business today without a web page?

Some are predicting that a giant economic Tsunami is imminent. One thing is sure. Riding the crest of that wave will be opportunity for those who recognize and seize it! In funeral service, there is no guarantee of *anything*, as we know it today. I shudder to think of it. I foresee a huge, government run mortuary up ahead with little or no love or compassion. I'm sure you're aware that many funeral homes

### 101 Battle Tested P/R Strategies for Successful Funeral Directors

are now offering reception centers where families can gather following the service, have refreshments and relax. Some funeral homes are already in the catering business. Consider combining that with your total grief recovery resource center. The possibilities are endless.

I suggest you try to get out ahead of the curve by introducing a total grief recovery resource center for your community. Focus on "grief recovery" as a key component of your service. Offer a combination book store, coffee shop and library. There's a whole raft of material available from the internet, your merchandise providers and the trade journals. *Loan* some of the grief recovery material, but make some available for sale for those who want their own. When you "loan" grief recovery material, you have a chance to talk with the person again when they return it. Invite them to join a grief recovery support group, or your widowed persons' social support group. Sponsor grief recovery workshops for police, and fire departments, veterans groups, service organizations, churches, or other groups like hairdressers, nursing home personnel, veterinarians, etc. mentioned in the book.

Start a memorial scrapbook with a page in it for each family you serve. Offer a one-on-one workshop to help families decorate their page. Display the scrapbooks prominently in your grief recovery center. In time these will become a valuable resource for your community, and a constant source of conversation for anyone that sees them: former residents, returning to visit, relatives from away, researching their genealogy, etc. will seek these scrapbooks out. Place a bulletin board in a conspicuous corner and encourage people to display photos of pets that have died. Sponsor periodical memorial services for those whose pets have died recently. Model them after the Life Appreciation Service.

Set up social meetings once a week at your center for clergy, clergy wives or husbands, police and fire department personnel, widows, widowers, kids, grieving pet owners, etc. You could make your room(s) available for widowed persons' social support groups. They could be used at different times by people with certain grief issues. In addition to organized support group meetings, people in grief could come and just socialize. (You will need a food handler's permit, anyway, so consider a coffee shop atmosphere, combined with a library-bookstore.) Then, for those interested, offer grief recovery support groups at different times. It would be a wonderful opportunity for widows and others who have recovered from their grief to volunteer as facilitators of these new groups. Remember to always have *two* facilitators for each group.

Become a high class coffee shop, with homemade pastries and good coffee. Let your resource center become the lounge for families using your funeral home for visiting hours. Offer free coffee to anyone from the funeral home that comes to the resource center to relax. Be sure and have laminated copies of the person's obituary available for sale at a low cost. (One free to the family.) Later, have video recordings of the actual funeral or memorial services, including a picture of each floral arrangement. This following may seem a little bit too much, but have your casket display, as well as your urn and vault displays, adjacent to your grief recovery resource center. Your competition is already displaying their merchandise at the malls. You want publicity and good public relations, This is a new concept. Think of the press and conversation throughout your community you will generate, once this is public knowledge. Think of all the people that will come in just to see the new grief recovery resource center, and go home and talk about it.

Email me if I can assist you in any way. Get in touch with me for your copy of my new Ebook for funeral directors. I call it "Orienting Toward Excellence (In Funeral Service)." 52 Winning P/R Strategies. PS. Lifetime mentoring goes with the book, too. Through the years you've helped your families face the initial shock and pain of the death of their loved ones. You've guided them over the roughest bump on their road to recovery. You've lovingly steered them around the worst pothole in their lives. You've earned their trust and respect, and provided an acceptable way for them to express their sorrow through memorialization. Why abandon them now? Take your professional service to its highest level. Be there for your families, *every* step of the way, until they have "*completely*" recovered.

Most families have no idea of what's ahead of them on that arduous road to recovery. They're at a complete loss as to what to do next (after the services). They're wide open for any suggestions you might offer. They trust *you* implicitly. They'd much rather have you or your staff help them, as they enter the post funeral stage of their grief, than someone they don't even know. Don't just thrust them out into the unknown without any guidance. Many will never receive support at all, if you do! I've heard stories I don't like about some grief recovery programs, and I've tried to put one together that answers everyones' questions honestly. Notice chapter five. It deals with questions many people ask about God. Some grief recovery support groups do not allow the subject of God to be discussed. I've found that God and heaven are usually the first things my groups *want* to talk about!

Whether or not you share the Christian faith, the chapter will give you straight answers about what the Bible says. If the family you are working with asks questions, offer them the references, and let them draw their own conclusions. Most people, Christian or not, still believe the Bible has straight answers.

When someone comes face to face with the reality that a loved one *is going* to die, and probably soon, there's no escaping it. They can't put it off. They have to deal with it, *right now*, ready or not. *Serious grieving begins immediately.* For a few days the person wanders around bewildered and scared. They may wonder if they're "losing it". Spurts of anger and gut wrenching depression have to be confronted. They're lonely. Often their family is scattered. There's little community support and only a few close friends understand what's happening. If they have visiting nurse services, hospice care may be offered with help for grieving.

In time, the grieving person winds up on *your* doorstep. Financial arrangements are made and the groundwork laid for a meaningful life appreciation service. That completed, most funeral planners usher the grieving person(s) out the door, where they flounder around helplessly, until the loved one actually dies. The trouble is, that person is grieving, *right now*. Their loved one may not die for weeks, or even months. During all that time, in some cases, all anyone who loves the person can do is *"stuff" their grief, anger and other feelings*. If someone is stuck in one of the potholes (talked about in chapter one), who's there to pull 'em out?

Before you abandon them to the wolves, spend a little extra time with them. Ask them if they have questions, concerns, or issues they want to talk about. Find out if there are pressing needs that have not been met. Ask if they'd like to get together with other people who are struggling with these same issues. Invite them to join *one of your new support groups*. Invite their family, too. They'll appreciate it. Check your mortuary trust files. You'll be amazed to find out that most of these families do not have an adequate support system either.

*"What I* really wish you'd do," my friend pleaded, "is start a support group for people who have to place a dying loved one in a nursing home." "That's it," I thought. "That's what funeral service needs! It's an opportunity to help people when they *begin* the grieving process. It's a brand spanking new idea that needs to be developed."

People who have loved ones who are dying need assurance that they've done *everything* they possibly could for them. Others who have wrestled with the same issues can be a real encouragement. It's comforting for them to know they're not alone—that caring people are willing to reach out and help them through this very difficult time. It's reassuring for them to know they can pick up the phone any time, day or night and talk with someone who's been there, and done that.

There are some great programs for families of those suffering with such things as cancer. Some of these support groups that functioned before the patient's death continue on with grief recovery programs after the patient dies. The ones I have heard of are facilitated by professionals such as LCSWs or nurses. Invite people who attend these groups to sit in on yours too. Remember, this program is not therapy or counseling, just common sense, down to earth, every day "stuff" that gets results.

There no better time for healing to begin. The loved one is still alive. There is still *time* to fix broken relationships; right any wrongs; make amends; ask forgiveness; to find out for sure the loved one's "real" thoughts and feelings about certain issues; to clear up misunderstandings, or to say "good bye" or "I love you." The loved one will almost certainly have things they need to say too. Others in a group can help the person sort those things out, and encourage one another to resolve the issues and deal with them one at a time.

A million dollars worth of public relations benefits are sailing right on by most funeral directors' door while they snooze in front of their TV. Your business is built on relationships, one individual at a time. A grief recovery program is the most effective *P/R* strategy there is, bar none. For my E-Book, "Orienting Toward Excellence (In Funeral Service). 52 Winning Strategies," E-mail me at pointtheway@myfairpoint.net. Free lifetime mentoring is also there for you.

## Beauticians—Hair Dressers—Barbers

Tanning Booth Operator, Manicurist or Cosmetologist

What kinds of problems will you be asked to help with today? Besides being an artist, entrepreneur, beauty consultant, manicurist and sales person, which of the following will you be expected to be qualified as? Financial consultant? Psychotherapist? Medical advisor? Interior decorator? Medical expert? Advisor to the lovelorn? Legal expert? Dietician? Wedding planner? Marriage counselor? <u>You're</u> the one the customer looks to for advice.

Someone once remarked to me that, in most cases, a hairdresser knows the customer better than her psychotherapist does.

When they're slighted socially, or jilted by a lover; when their teenager turns belligerent; when they're passed over for the promotion, they think they should have had; when their house is foreclosed on; or they are forced to tear themselves up by the roots and leave family and friends, <u>you're</u> the one they look to for comfort and understanding. You're closer than most family. From everything I know about beauticians (and I know a lot of them) you do a *darned good* job steering everyone around the potholes in their road to recovery!

However, do you fumble for words when you look into a customer's eyes and realize that what you thought they were having was a bad hair day, and it turns out to *really be a gut wrenching crisis, like;*

* "My kid's got terminal cancer."
* "My husband just ran off with another woman, or man."
* "My teenager is going to prison for dealing in drugs."
* "My best friend just dropped dead."

Are you prepared for the _really_ tough ones? *Of course*, you're going to pray with them! But after that? This book can't give you better advice than you already know to do instinctively. Now, you'll never have to wonder what to say after that, or ponder how to take them around (or through) the potholes that lie ahead.

All too often you find yourself working with a customer who is _recently_ widowed. This must be the most difficult part of your job! You're probably the first one outside of her immediate family to console her. I trust the information in this book has helped you recognize where she is in the grieving process. If what she's doing and saying is normal, or if she really needs professional help RIGHT AWAY, because she thinks she might be "losing" it. You will be able to offer her the best advice anyone can give her, because of your added insight and experience. As time goes on and your customer has to work through the recovery process, one issue at a time, you will receive the inner strength, confidence and self assurance *you* need to be effective.

This material will not only have given you a place to start, but it will be a guide to help you walk *with* your customer *step by step* as she struggles through the *entire* grief recovery process, weeks and even months down the road.

You've probably seen it often, and understand *better than anyone*, the pressure on the *newly* widowed person. She's hurting. There's quite often long distances between surviving family members, leaving the widow alone and disconnected. There's less support from the community than a few years ago. Her social life has changed radically. Many of her friends don't know what to say so they avoid her, and say nothing. Close friends who are married shun her because they don't want a single woman anywhere near their husband.

If you know two or more women that have been widowed within the past couple of years, this book will show you how to start a social group for them. (Or a grief recovery support group. if they are not ready for anything social.) Chapter 6 takes you step by step through the process, if you want to organize either type of group. God bless you. I don't have to tell you there is a world of hurting people out there crying out to you! Don't hesitate to contact me if I can help you. Free lifetime mentoring goes with the purchase of the book.

## Police, Fire Departments, Veterans Groups, Military Chaplains

When I think of strategy I'm reminded of the Bible story of David the shepherd boy and Goliath, the most feared military commander of his time. Goliath was ten feet tall, had the best armor made, the fiercest army in the world behind him, and all of his enemies were "terrified". The account is in First Samuel chapter seventeen.

David did not fear. He recognized the enemy's most vulnerable spot, used the element of surprise, deployed a secret weapon and brought the giant crashing to the ground. Our enemy, the devil, whose mission is to kill steal and destroy, has likely just won a battle with one or more of your people. Like the giant, grief is probably towering over them and you. Fear, which is Satan's most effective weapon, seems to be overtaking everyone.

Remember, a Christian's armor is better than his. We wear the belt of truth, the breastplate of righteousness, the helmet of salvation and our shoes are fitted to spread the gospel of peace. Our shield of faith is able to deflect his flaming missiles. God has given us the sword of the spirit which is the Word of God. Instead of one, we have two secret weapons—love and forgiveness. We also have been given the radar to maneuver around the potholes the devil has placed in the road to recovery.

Every effective organization I know of has support groups. The army calls them squads. (When I was in, a squad was nine men.) The Communist cell group was ten. Many churches have small home Bible studies. One Christian denomination uses what they call a "divide and multiply" strategy. When a home group reaches (?) 9 they split, and form two groups. You probably have teams within your department.

The purpose of the grief recovery support group program is to introduce recovery principles to the facilitators of existing groups so they will be able to help someone (or the whole group) that is faced with a loss, or crisis, to cope. They can encourage them, and help them through the grieving process, and pick up the slack, if the one grieving is unable to function normally. Eventually, everyone reads the book and is able to empower others.

That's a great concept, and I highly recommend you embrace it. So organize your groups. Pick someone that will commit to reading this book and put the grief recovery principles to work. A widowed person has a much better understanding of other peoples' feelings. Try and find someone in your organization who has been widowed for some time, and who has pretty much resolved their own grief issues before giving them a leadership role. This is the ideal person to assume the leadership role in your new grief recovery program. That person recognizes the potholes (in chapter one) and has managed to free themselves from most of them. Ask him or her to pick an assistant and let them set a time each week for the meetings. I've found that no matter what anyone is grieving for, or about, the recovery process is very similar. Identify each issue. Get it out in the light of day. Help *everyone* express their feelings. Guide them through closure(completing their relationships) and move on. If necessary, revisit the issue again and again until the person grieving can truly put it behind them. If you find your group is dealing with a real crisis, such as the death of a fellow group member, get your professionals in there at once. They will have had training in counseling and therapy. This material is for the long haul. Chapter two explains what you will be dealing with if a crisis situation does present itself unexpectedly, and it is wise for everyone to understand it.

You will be amazed how quickly strong bonds develop between members of a support group. There are exceptions to every situation, especially if men and women work closely together. My experience in grief recovery support groups has been with women only (exceptions being, with support groups for grieving parents). Chapter three deals with that subject extensively. People are less candid in mixed groups, and it is imperative that trust and confidentiality develop to the max. Certain work environments may go more smoothly by mixing, but beware of the sexual harassment issue, or illicit sexual relationships developing.

I don't know how to deal with the issue of a person feeling guilty that his or her life has been spared and another was taken in an accident. The only advice I can offer is: "God has a job for you to do. Don't wallow around in guilt or self pity! There is *nothing we can do to change the past.*" If your support group can't help, seek a Christian psychotherapist or clergy person. To police chiefs: For suggestions regarding public relations and reaching out to the public, go to "Possibilities," or "Police Departments," at the end of this chapter.

## Church Groups

*At Last: A Christ Centered Grief Recovery Program For Your Church.*

Pastor: How many times have you prayed, *"Lord, show me a more excellent way to meet the emotional and spiritual needs of those I serve, who are grieving."*

*Rejoice, your prayers have been answered!*

Here's great news! God has just flung open a wondrous window of opportunity for His church, and presented us with an enormous frontier for ministry. Even now, I believe He's placing the Pioneer Spirit in His people to explore it and tame it for Him! The new frontier is right in *your* own church, *your* neighborhood and *your* community. *I Believe This Is The Finest Opportunity To Evangelize, That The Modern Church Has Ever Had!*

### Thomas Anonymous

It's a volunteer-operated, grief recovery program that will bond your people more closely together, enhance your P/R and, over time, significantly improve church attendance. Solid friendships and fierce loyalties develop, as one person is encouraged and supported by others in the group.

I couldn't believe what I was hearing! The leadership of some very popular grief recovery programs refuse to talk about God or Jesus at their support group meetings! In every group I've been involved with, *people want to talk about God!* They need to know that He *didn't* take their loved one from them or cause "it" to happen. (See chapter five).

When does a Bible study or other meeting become a grief recovery support group? The minute a member has a crisis: a serious family issue, a teen problem, a fractured relationship, or a serious illness. We need to be able to respond positively, on the spot.

Invite other groups in your area to meet at your church, and share these grief recovery techniques with them. Start groups for families who have lost their homes through fire or foreclosure or unemployment. Offer assistance with food and necessities. If your veterans do not have support groups offer them. Offer them to military families during a deployment. Veterans from the Korean and Vietnam wars are still hurting. Veterans groups are struggling financially during this prolonged economic depression. Consider making your facilities available to them. It will take a committee to structure some rules, but by helping them, they could help your church immensely. You haven't got to go far to find people who are hurting Consider support groups for families whose loved ones are struggling with addictions. Many churches allow AA and Al-anon groups to use their facilities.

Families of people who are incarcerated badly need a support network. Why not reach out to them in Christian love? These people are certainly grieving, and are very likely in need of financial assistance. Resources may be available from Chuck Colson's Prison Fellowship.

As I pointed out in chapter three, there's a real need for support groups for women who have miscarried! I was astounded when I found out that *every* one of the women in one grief recovery support group had miscarried *at least once*. *Quietly* spread the word that you are starting a group for women who would like closure. In so many instances, extended family and friends don't even know about the pregnancy. The mother's feelings are usually not taken into consideration, and she is unable to even express her feelings, let alone have meaningful closure. The prevailing thought is usually, "Oh, she can always have another child." Many women are able to recover and do just fine. However, there are some who do serious grieving. (Sometimes for the rest of their lives!) They have bonded with the child and don't know how to complete their relationship with it. The same thing applies to families of stillborn children(families of children who died prior to birth.) Your church could make it known to OB/GYN clinics, maternity wards at hospitals, funeral homes, and others who work with pregnant women, that you have grief recovery support groups, and would welcome women who are trying to deal with these kinds of issues. You can fill a huge void. At the same time you are putting Christianity in shoe leather for them.

There are exceptions to everything, but I certainly do *not* recommend you work with women who have had abortions. You are probably aware of the intense feelings of guilt some of these women are suffering. Reach out to the pro-life groups in your area. Share the information in this book. Provide grief recovery workshops for them. They will almost certainly welcome your concern. They may provide support groups, but probably do not understand grief recovery dynamics. Nonprofessional facilitators should not try to run a support group of this nature. However, the closure and grief recovery information provided in the book could be very helpful to facilitators working with these mothers (and possibly dads).

Wake up, tune in. Seize the moment! Fill the vacuum! These are blessings in disguise. Most other support groups are <u>no</u>t offering Christ, or even mentioning God. The benefits for your church are <u>enormous</u>. Remember, these are only grief recovery support groups, not therapy or professional counseling sessions. After reading the book, people will have a much better understanding of when someone needs to be referred to clergy or a professional psychotherapist.

These *are the times when people are more open to the Gospel than at any other time in their lives!* There's a wonderful window of opportunity being flung open before us, to proclaim Christ in a loving, non-threatening way to <u>all</u> who are grieving anthing.

A little further on in this chapter is an outline for integrating grief recovery techniques into a Junior or High School curriculum. Public schools do not take kindly to anything that mentions God or Jesus Christ. The material presents a marvelous way to proclaim Christ, and talk about spiritual things with students. This is your opportunity to empower them for a lifetime of service to anyone grieving.

Almost anyone with a heart for the Lord can be trained as a facilitator. The ideal situation is for two facilitators to work together as a team with groups of four or five. However, one-on-one mentoring works very well. Never do this alone with anyone of the opposite sex! Loan the material to someone you trust and ask them to assist you.

There are always people who want to talk about seemingly minor issues with their pastor. This sometimes places an unreasonable demand on the clergy person's time. Support groups can relieve at least some of that pressure. The clergyperson and the facilitator need to be on the same spiritual frequency, and have periodical meetings. Confidentialities should never be shared, but the clergyperson should know that the facilitator is dealing with a particularly difficult issue within the group. People in support groups can talk about a whole lot of issues that fall under the heading "grief related," and a solid Christian facilitator can help tremendously. Again, each group should not only have one facilitator, but another person, who is solid in their faith, that acts as assistant facilitator. Eventually, as several support groups become active, the clergy person will want to have periodical meetings with all the facilitators and assistants.

*Starting a church-oriented support group:*

Most people enjoy being in a group. I had no problem getting different groups started just by inviting people who I thought were hurting to sit in. Finding a *time* for men to meet is a whole different story. One Bible study-support group for men meets at 6:00 AM Saturday mornings. Within the past two years we have been able to mentor five new Christians. I have been at successful men's groups that met for lunch once a week. Refer to chapter six on forming groups. The best advice I can give is, if you know anyone who is hurting, explain to them that you are willing to start a group and ask that person to help you find others who would like to sit in. They likely know others with similar issues. If relief is in sight they'll *want* to help.

The church setting is probably the easiest place to get a group started. It is critical that they know you are not doing it alone, and that they feel safe. It was often harder to find a convenient time for everyone to attend meetings than to organize the group itself. Be very careful that you don't cram your faith down people's throats, if they don't agree with you 100% on everything spiritual. I was usually able to *temporarily* side step most difficult questions. Rather than take the chance of getting someone mad at me for contradicting them right then, or embarrassing them in front of others, when they brought up a difficult subject, I felt it was better to back off. If I came across as too strong, I might lose the one who needed the group the most.

What has worked well for me, is this: When someone has thrown me a curve, such as reincarnation, I would not let it visibly shake me. I would not make a big issue out of it at the time. I would calmly say, "I'll bring in some material on that next week," or, "Let me see what the Bible says about that, and I'll bring it in next week."

After I completed my homework, I would type out an informational sheet, make copies, and *give it to everyone at the end of the next meeting.* This gives everyone the chance to read over the material during the following week, and refresh their minds as to what the Bible really does say. I would tell the group, "We'll talk about this next time." Doing it this way, the person that asked the question is not embarrassed. Be sure and start the next meeting off with the material. (Have extra copies in case someone has misplaced theirs.)

I've found that people need to express their opinions without being embarrassed. They need to ask perplexing questions in a *safe environment* and not get shot down. Instead of over-reacting to way-out philosophies, such as, "In my next life

I'm going to come back as—." or, "I went to this fortune teller, and she said—." etc. If the person is put down, they very likely will not come back to another meeting. When I start a new support group, I let everyone know they are free to ask any question, but the Bible is the final authority. Always speak in love.

*Everything is kept strictly confidential at the meetings.* The facilitator needs to remind everyone from time to time that it *is* being honored.

I start right out with a paper for everyone giving the list of everyone in the group, and their telephone numbers. I list these things (above), state emphatically that this group is not about counseling or therapy. I make it clear that their questions will be dealt with *first*, and there is no specific agenda, or date to end. I also let it be understood that my goal is to "empower you to help others to become facilitators." Then, depending on whether or not I think the person is ready to lead a group, I give them essentially a copy of this material. Then, I ask the one that I feel would "fit in best", to sit in as an assistant to me. Right now as I write this, I am ready to go with a second year of the medically related issues, support group, and the assistant will take over as the lead facilitator.

Never talk in a condescending way (put down) to anyone. Most of us have been out in left field on one Biblical issue or another. We were all "babes in the woods" sometime. In chapter five, I have explained many points that have been asked me over the years regarding God, Jesus, heaven and the Bible. There are Biblical references to back everything up that I have said.

There are so many issues where grief is a dominating factor. Over the years I have been broadsided with people dealing with miscarriage, parent abandonment, husband leaving a family destitute, teen issues, serious personal illness, illness of parents, spouses or close relatives, sexual abuse, death of a spouse or parent's death, divorce, fractured relationships, and various combinations of all of the above. These situations were a lot easier for me to deal with, knowing the underlying issue for most everyone suffering with them was grief, *intense grief.* In some of these situations, many people dealing with these issues did not even realize the issues were still unresolved from their past. I've learned to take just one issue at a time and deal with that. Wait until another session, when that one person is talking, and then I approach another issue, and deal with that one.

I'm happy to say, Jesus Christ still changes lives! He is faithful. The satisfaction of being able to point hurting people to Him, and help them get rid of that awful load of grief they were carrying around is indescribable! **If your church has an education program, there is more information later in this chapter on applying the material to a church school setting.**

## Support Groups for Those with Serious Medical Issues.

Everything was going along beautifully with my grief recovery support groups when I found myself facing a personal medical crisis. I had been battling Macular Degeneration for a few years and suddenly realized that it had deteriorated to Wet Macular Degeneration (WM D). I came very close to not having my driver's license renewed and found myself grieving. Grieving my loss of health, grieving my possible loss of freedom, and just plain feeling sorry for myself.

Some of the women in my grieving groups had serious medical issues, but until it happened to *me*, I had not considered facilitating a group just for suffering people. It took me about two days to get seven women to agree to sit in on the first group. I think the real motivation was to be able to help others, rather than to be supported in their own discomfort. It was ironic. One of them had just been diagnosed with diabetes and was having a really hard time coping. Miraculously, another in the group had been battling diabetes for years and knew all the ropes. She took the newly diagnosed woman under her wing and coached and encouraged her the rest of the time we met.

Please allow me to restate my insistence that you do not try to facilitate a group alone. The woman who helped me had been through the grief recovery program and had developed a deep insight into and sensitivity to where the others were coming from. She spent hours at a time praying for each of them. Several times she suggested we pray together a certain way. I often forgot she was even there and jumped in ahead of her when she really had more understanding of what was happening (and what to say) than I did. She was a wonderful asset.

About two months after we began, one of the women came to me and said, in effect, that several of them wanted to pursue a more aggressive approach spiritually. I had purposely avoided doing that and had followed the basic grief recovery format. I didn't want to offend anyone and have them not show up. I must have had an inspired moment because I asked this lady to show me the direction she wanted to go by leading the group the following week. She accepted willingly and it was a resounding success. Each week after that, the women took turns sharing what had helped them get through their difficult moments.

In one way or another each one acknowledged that the grieving process is necessary in dealing with their medical issues. Realization that others were trying to cope with the same issues and having someone to talk with between meetings was a positive factor. Some of the Scripture that was shared is found in chapter five.

May the Lord Jesus Christ, who serves with wounded hands, teach you to serve others. May the Lord Jesus Christ, who loves with a wounded heart, Be your love forever. Bless God wherever you go, May everyone we meet, see the face of Jesus in us. (Modified prayer of Rev. Merv. Lanctot)

If you have a church school, see the section on schools later in this chapter.

## Veterinarians

Trainers, Pet Stores, etc. If you're not a Vet, but have a pet, loan this book to your favorite Vet. Point out this section. You'll have a friend.

No one can argue that in many households a pet is treated like another person. When death occurs the trauma is as real as if it had been a human that died. When someone brings their pet to you for euthanizing or cremation, there's a lot more that could be done to help them through the grieving process(or a lot more than was done when my pet died several years ago).

Understanding that the pet owner's grief is very real, a few more minutes spent with them talking about their pet would be very helpful. Even asking them if they want to spend a few minutes with their pet and say the things they need to say *to them* would be very therapeutic.

Invite the pet owner to a support group in a couple of weeks. It would give them a new focus and take their mind off themselves. Pattern the support group exactly as you would for a support group for widows, parents or anyone else needing support. Knowing others are grieving the death of their own pet will be beneficial. Friendships will develop. This is something a Veterinarian's Assistant or a dedicated volunteer can do, and do very well. You can provide the benefit by offering your waiting room once a month. For example this could pave the way for a Pet Pals club, a group to establish a hiking trail for dogs, or an occasional pet rally with a picnic, games, other activities, and fellowship. You may want to consider organizing a bird dog or Beagle club, a workshop, or field day. Your P/R will sky rocket!

I'm aware of several veterinarians who will go to a pet owner's home and euthanize their pet when the time comes. You could combine this with a farewell service for the pet, with family members, close friends, and neighbors present. Chapter three on family issues has several other suggestions.

Most families that want to do this would willingly pay for your time (or your assistant's) to facilitate this type of group. The information they need is in this book.

I highly recommend you have memorial services for pet owners from time to time, especially during the holidays. Consider giving each person who brings a pet to you for any reason, a handout with that information included.

A press release and perhaps a paid announcement in the daily newspaper a week before each service would likely bring people who are not regular customers to the service. Help them remember their pet in a meaningful way. You could also make a pass out and give it to each pet owner using your other professional services. Something like this. "Memorial services for grieving pet owners (and family). Third Monday each month at 4:00 PM. in our waiting room. Please call for confirmation." Sponsor a public memorial service for grieving pet owners around the holidays. Decorate a Christmas tree, with an ornament for each pet being remembered, or have a candle lighting service, with small scented candle as a memorial keepsake. Ask each owner to read an obituary type tribute to (for) each pet.

Place a large bulletin board in your waiting room for anyone to post a photo of their deceased pet. Set a time limit of several months, then take them down and hold them for pets' families to pick up so anyone viewing it would have a sense that it's OK to mourn the death of a pet. Post dates for memorial services on that bulletin board.

If there is any farmland, or wooded area outside of the residential area in your community you might want to lease some of it and develop an exercise path for pets. Again this would be an ideal project for a new pet owners' social club. Sanitary materials are probably available for purchase through your local public works department. Lease with the option to buy, as you may want to develop a pet cemetery or memorial park. PS: Do you have a periodic newsletter to your community at large? Contact me if you want help or ideas.

## Schools

You know so much better than I do the horrific situations many kids are living with every day like drugs, alcohol, and abuse. Is it possible that at least some of the behavioral and learning problems they have might be grief related? My folks were divorced during my preschool years and it affected my actions, my school work, and everything I did right through Junior High. Please, ask yourself, if a couple of hours each week, working with a troubled child in a one-on-one setting would be worth the time investment a few years down the road?

Perhaps by using the strategy in the book, teachers would be able to identify that problem if its grief related and either nip it in the bud, or refer the child for professional help. Often, children think they are responsible for a bad situation at home, such as divorce, or abuse, and carry that extra load of guilt, in addition to the grief that's already tormenting them.

I do not believe support groups for identifying and helping children with grief related problems are practical. Sessions can get too emotional, and kids tend to divulge confidentiality issues much too frequently. I do believe the way to go is for teachers to establish grief recovery techniques into the groups they may already have for themselves, and even form special grief recovery support groups as suggested in chapter six.

Using the information in chapters one and two, teachers and guidance counselors can identify, and to some degree, help troubled children. Just understanding how to help a child on a one to one basis is all I think a teacher can do. For a child to know they have someone who cares, that they can come to when the going gets tough, is priceless. We sometimes forget that delayed grief can be a significant factor in anyone's behavior (chapter two). I did not grieve the loss of my mother (at about age five), until I was a senior in High School. It was years before I understood why I was grieving so intensely for a classmate who had been killed in an accident. Just being able to express the gut-wrenching emotions bottled up inside some of these kids would relieve a lot of their stress. It would also affect everyone around.

There is no way anyone, including teachers, can leave an undealt with problem at home! They bring it with them, wherever they go, like carrying a heavy load on their shoulders. Recognizing it, talking about it, sorting out their options, venting their emotions, even crying or raging, saying what's bothering them and *having someone who cares, with whom they can talk* confidentially will relieve a lot of pressure.

Your people may be well equipped to deal with grief related problems. If so, congratulations. If not, would you be able to invest a couple of hours a week, working with a troubled child, using proven grief recovery techniques? I'm not talking about therapy, or counseling by professionals. What I've had experience with is everyday common sense, down to earth "stuff" that gets results, and is explained in this book. Over the years I've worked with widows, grieving parents and people dealing with all kinds of grief related issues. I believe the same principles could help in a school environment. Pick and choose whatever you like about the contents of chapters one and two. If one teacher can use one technique, or identify one child who is grieving, and help him or her, I have accomplished something. I can only visualize a lot less stress in the classroom. You have an overwhelming task daily, and I commend you for the great job you do.

With the current anti-Christian bias in most schools today, this program would probably only apply to private, Christian, and home school groups. Anyway, for those educators with a pioneer spirit, here's how to get started. I will gladly help anyone. I don't have to tell you that when a tragedy, like the death of a child, or a teacher strikes a school, everyone needs a way to express their feelings, to say the things they need to say, and grieve appropriately. You need to turn to the professionals. After the professionals have left, this material offers a practical, *long term approach that* gets results.

Here are some suggestions on how to organize a meaningful Life Appreciation Service when someone has died. The school may already have plans in place. If so that's wonderful.

**A Life Appreciation Service**: It's important for any school to have some kind of service at the school for a deceased student or teacher. Most funeral directors today are familiar with creating a meaningful life appreciation service using appropriate displays of personal items, PowerPoint photo presentations, and other items that will help everyone remember the deceased person as they knew him or her. Displaying some of the deceased person's personal things in a school setting would be extremely helpful. The first thing I would suggest you do is appoint someone who knew the deceased child well to be the contact person between the school and the family, as well as the funeral home. Probably the Principal, or a teacher who knew the student well should be with the student that contacts the family. Whether or not arrangements are completed for public services, both the funeral home and the family should be aware that the school is also planning some type of service at the school. Some of the student's family may want to attend the school service, so be sure times are coordinated.

Understanding this will prevent duplication of effort. A meaningful display on PowerPoint for example, or things like a deceased child's fish pole, guitar or hobby items can be used at both services, and public visiting hours too. Discs with favorite songs recorded on them could be used at both the school and funeral home. If the family knows you will want items that will help everyone remember the deceased child as they knew him or her, it will allow the family to coordinate the displays, and PowerPoint, simultaneously.

Students should know ASAP that services will be held at the school in addition to whatever is planned by the family and funeral home. Plan to have the school memorial service soon, while particulars involving the death are still on student's minds.

The next thing I would suggest is identifying several other students who were friendly with the deceased child. Solicit their help putting together a meaningful service. They will know what music the deceased child enjoyed, his or her hobbies, likes, dislikes, etc. and could say some appropriate things at the service. It would be appropriate to ask these kids to suggest three or four (max) friends to speak at the service, and require that they write out what they plan to say for review beforehand.

Pass out a keepsake program with the child's picture on it to everyone who attends the services. Have extra ones in case some student didn't get one, and the family might want several to send to relatives and friends from away.

If it's possible, have photos enlarged and create a collage where everyone will see them as they enter for the services. If the child rode his or her bike often, that would be appropriate to display. I-pods, texting devices or their boom box would add character to the display. Many kids like to play musical instruments so if this child did, have his or her instrument on display. If the child liked to go camping, an acorn, a pine twig, or a marshmallow, wrapped in tinfoil with a ribbon would remind others of the child's love of a campfire, and roasted marshmallows. All of this would help everyone remember the child as they knew him or her. A music group from the school might play or sing the deceased's favorite song. Be sure the words are appropriate! The school bands could play the school song, and at least one patriotic song, too. Ask each person at the service to write a few words of comfort for the family. Collect and deliver them after the services.

If the child was involved in any sports activity, invite the team or group to come in uniform and sit together. If he or she was involved in a youth group at their church, it might be appropriate for the group leader to say a few words. Many older teens volunteer at soup kitchens, food pantries, etc. A representative from wherever the child volunteered could be invited to speak. Of course if the child was involved in scouting, Civil Air Patrol, or summer camp, someone or something from that organization should take part or be mentioned. Don't allow too many speakers. They tend to repeat what others before them have said, so ask each one that will speak, to limit their time to just a few minutes.

If the child enjoyed a particular place, like the skate board park, everyone could be given a balloon and asked to release them together at that place immediately following the service. If the child rode horseback, it would be appropriate to have the saddled horse standing a short distance from the burial lot, or outside the school as people enter or leave the premises. Display anything unique or different, like the family camper, their dad's bass boat, if they liked to fish, or their motorcycle if they liked to ride. Try and get as many friends involved in making the services as meaningful as possible. Three little boys died in a fire. Following services for them, nearly every-one in town turned out at the train station and released brightly colored balloons as the train slowly arrived. These kids loved the train, and apparently had ridden on it at some time or other. *Any service that lasts more than an hour is too long.*

Unlike in the case of personal losses, special grief recovery support groups for friends of the deceased child should be considered, beginning ASAP and continuing several weeks or more following the service. Any child who wants to be in the support group can attend. Re-read the items on "delayed grief" in chapter two. Be aware that some children with other deep-seated grief issues may be helped by a grief support group for the deceased child's friends.

*If it is a teacher* who has died, many of these suggestions could be modified, but the students should be allowed to say good-bye in one form or another.

## Clubs, Fraternities, Groups, Teams.

Everything that applies to a service at a child's school applies to organizations. A special time of remembrance could be arranged, with or without the family present. Some kind of memorial plaque could be presented to the family, at the service. If there were close friends, perhaps the leader could facilitate a special support group a few weeks after the services. Even though there may have been a public service, and your organization took part, or attended as a body, I encourage a service for members at your own meeting place. Invite several friends to give eulogies.

A lodge or club is a "safe" place to have a support group. Reach out and invite members from other groups that the deceased person was involved with to take part in your support group. There's always a chance the others participating will want to become members of your organization.

## Possibilities

When we have a need and someone helps us, *we instinctively want to return the favor.* When someone is carrying around a load of grief, and we help them get rid of it, words can't describe how much it will be appreciated, or the *personal satisfaction you* will receive.

In a work environment, your staff will reward you with increased dedication, commitment and professional excellence. There's a world of hurting people out there, with various grief issues weighing them down. You'll find just what you need to help them right here. The sooner they get the load of grief off their backs the smoother things will go.

Is it possible that Insurance Companies, Underwriters, etc: might want to embark on an entirely new public relations strategy? For example, would fire insurance companies consider launching support groups for homeowners whose homes have been ravaged by fire? These people are grieving for all kinds of reasons. Here are a few issues that might be dealt with: knowing how to restore partially damaged furniture that has sentimental value; the best ways to go about securing temporary living arrangements; how to deal with financial crisis; help finding temporary pet boarding; support groups for kids dealing with loss of special keepsakes or pets destroyed in the blaze; and how to help folks cope with family members who were burned or injured. If family members lost their lives, there definitely would be an opportunity to offer long term grief recovery support groups.

What are the possibilities of getting people together to grieve the loss of family valuables, keepsake jewelry and family heirlooms? There is a feeling of having been violated following break-ins and robberies. Learning how others have coped with the loss would be helpful, and for those who are recovering, being able to offer helpful suggestions and encouragement would be a wonderful.

Fire departments could set up support groups for families in their area, possibly in conjunction with neighboring towns. They could also work with fire insurance companies to establish support groups.

Police Departments: In addition to establishing in-house grief recovery support groups, why not offer support groups to people who have been raped, or assaulted, parents of kids in trouble? When my son was in trouble with the law my wife and I were grieving big time. All through the time he was in prison, and during the rehabilitation process we were grieving. When another family found out my son was involved in drugs they sought us out just to talk. With so many kids on drugs today, why not offer a support groups for the parents. (Maybe one for the kids themselves.) Take a look at the widower support group section in chapter six. Is it possible to borrow some of the ideas and projects from that program, and adapt them to a youth rehabilitation program?

I can never remember a time when police departments needed support of the public more than today. These groups are intended for families of victims, and families of prisoners, but knowing you are really there to help rehabilitate felons, and support their families while that is happening, will build a good-will/ public relations framework that will reach out into the grass roots of the community at large. It will take time and commitment, but most programs that are worthwhile do.

What about Banks and Credit Unions?

How about support groups for homeowners trying to cope with foreclosures?

Employment agencies:

Wouldn't people trying to find work in this troubled economy find comfort in a support group? Would a group be a way to get acquainted with potential clients?

## Review

There are many people grieving all kinds of issues. I see the church being the best source of support, but I am sure businesses dealing with people who are grieving could improve their public relations by offering various types of support groups. I have found that people dealing with different kinds of grief issues will easily bond with others dealing with entirely different issues. The grieving process is very similar regardless of what it is we are grieving for.

If there are things between you and a loved one who has died that you were unable to complete, or if there are things you did not get to say to them that you wish you could say, *PICTURE THAT PERSON IN YOUR MIND'S EYE AND SAY WHAT YOU NEED TO SAY TO THAT PERSON RIGHT NOW.* If you need forgiveness, ask that person for it, and then ask God to forgive you. If the person needs forgiveness from you, give it to them. You will not heal in your soul if there is unforgiveness, or guilt! If you cannot bring yourself to 'say' what you need to, or if you have trouble visualizing the person in your mind's eye, write a letter to the person. Write everything you want to say in the letter. THEN TEAR THE LETTER UP. HOLDING THE PIECES OF PAPER IN YOUR HAND, PRAY OVER THE LETTER. TAKE THE WHOLE SITUATION TO JESUS. ASK HIM TO INTERCEDE FOR YOU WITH THAT PERSON. THEN ASK HIM TO FILL YOU WITH ALL THE LOVE AND FORGIVENESS THAT HE HAD FOR THE ONES THAT CRUCIFIED HIM, WHEN HE SAID "FATHER, FORGIVE THEM, FOR

**Thomas Anonymous**

THEY KNOW NOT WHAT THEY ARE DOING." When you have completely satisfied yourself that the matter is completed, burn or bury the torn-up letter. You will be able to walk away free. At this point healing will begin. I feel that it is important to get someone that is seriously grieving into some kind of support after a few months. Is it better to have, say a widow, with someone that has been divorced, or dealing with someone that has a terminal illness? I can't give you a straight answer. It pretty much depends on the individuals, and how well they know each other. As much as possible I would get people with similar issues in the same groups. I think you are better to have two small groups with similar issues, rather than one larger group with different issues.

People in grief are self-centered, and I find they often get irritated if someone with an issue different than theirs gets talking about their issues.

Once again I want to remind you that you are welcome to contact me by Email if you want someone to talk with. There is no charge.

**pointtheway@myfairpoint.net**

## Section Five

# Why God, Why?

I've never seen it fail. When dealing with grief, _**the subject of God always comes up**_! I can't imagine having a grief recovery support group without allowing people to talk about God at some point; yet many facilitators refuse to allow their participants to bring up the subject. In my opinion, understanding God and the Bible is **THE** most critical part of the recovery process.

**Here are some things about death and the Christian faith that people are often unclear about. The Bible is the final authority. This Is a good reference point when you have folks that need straight answers about God, pets dying, reincarnation and where to go for Biblical answers.**

Many people toss flowery words around, trying to make a grieving person feel better. Expressions such as, "God needed another little angel," or, "God needed another pretty flower in His flower garden," are common. People of faith often ask, "Why did God take my loved one? _Hundreds_ of Christians were praying for him or her!" They very often ask, "Why did God let this terrible thing happen? God is supposed to be a God of love!" One woman asked angrily,

"Where was God when *my* son was killed?" A wise person answered, "right where He was when they killed **His** son."

Are you one of those people that believe everybody is going to heaven? Will you concede that perhaps Hitler and a few choice terrorists *might* not make it? As to whether a loved one is or isn't there, is not for us to judge. I would never even hint that anyone's loved one is not in heaven. A few months before the vilest man I ever knew died, Jesus changed his life! Only God knows for certain if a person's heart is right with Him. Jesus would not have had to come into the world, live a perfect life, and die a horrible death to pay the price for our sins, if everybody was going to heaven anyway. Jesus paid a terrible price so we could be with Him. Would you agree that each one of us sin from time to time, and we have mean, hateful, impure thoughts that need forgiveness? There are situations in our lives where we need help. dealing with?

The Bible says that *it's appointed unto man once to die* and after that the judgment. (**Hebrews, chapter 1: verse # 27**) No one knows the time of someone's death. People abuse themselves for years; smoking, drinking, taking drugs, and subtly abusing their bodies, then wonder why God doesn't instantly step in and heal them. To say God ***never*** heals anyone who has abused themselves, is to deny God's power and sovereignty. Sometimes He overrides His own laws. WE CAN'T PUT GOD IN A BOX.

He has promised never to give us more than we can handle, with His help. He's closer than a brother to His people during their darkest hour. His Holy Spirit is the Comforter. In time, God will ***always*** make some good come out of *every* bad situation. In the first book of the Bible, God gives us a promise. "If you love ME, I will bless you." God judges the heart. I believe that many people have a change of heart toward God when they realize they are actually going to die soon.

The Bible says that no one can **earn** their way into heaven, **buy** their way in, or **be good enough** to get there. **Heaven is a free gift** and all anyone has to do is accept that gift by faith. **Ephesians chapter two** says "For it is by free grace (God's unmerited favor) that we are saved (delivered from judgment and made partakers of Christ's salvation) through (your) faith. And this (salvation) is not of yourselves (of your own doing, it came not through your own striving) but it is the gift of God; Not because of works (not the fulfillment of the Law's demands}, lest any man should boast. {It is not the result of what anyone can possibly do, so no one can pride himself in it or take glory to himself.}

Many people believe that they have to "earn" their way into heaven; if they do "good" works, and are morally straight that they will get there. This passage of scripture tells us very plainly that Jesus is the way. In the book of (Romans, Chapter 10: verse 13) it says "For everyone who calls on the name of the Lord [invoking Him as Lord} will be saved. **JESUS**! You're saved.

Death is a lot easier to understand when we realize that each of us is a spirit being, living in a body. Our spirit never dies. Only our body dies and eventually returns to dust. (To be raised up on the last day.) We have a soul. It has three parts: our mind (the brain is the computer), our emotions, and the one thing no other animal has, **a free will**. We make the choice of whether or not to love and serve God.

Many believe that once a Christian, always a Christian. That anyone that is a Christian will automatically go to heaven. That's not true. Keep reading. No one can take salvation away from a Christian, but they sure can throw it away! Don't get discouraged. We get into this a little later in the chapter.

**Do little children *always* go to heaven when they die?** I believe they do. There is a time in everyone's life when we intentionally choose to do what is evil and reject God, or to love God and serve Him. Little kids can't make that choice. Jesus said "The kingdom of God belongs to little children." Years ago, a doctor's words made a lasting impression on me. A small child (two or three years old) had been killed in a farm accident. I remember the doctor lovingly saying to the parents, "What a sad place heaven would be, if there were no little children there."

**Was it God's will that my loved one die?** *No one* has all the answers. Even the ones who think they do! Sometimes there are factors nobody but God knows about. Some go back many years, even generations. It's easy to blame everything on God, but there are natural laws in place that God usually does not override.

One of the devil's favorite strategies is to cause pain and suffering; then make people think God did it. Here are a few Scriptures from the Bible that tell us *plainly* that God is not to blame for sickness, disease or suffering. **(Job Chapter one)** clearly says the devil is behind disasters. **(Hebrews 2: 16)** He Himself (Jesus) suffered physical pain and mental anguish. **(John 10: 10)** Jesus said, "The thief (devil) comes to kill, steal and destroy. I came so that they may have life and have it in abundance. I lay down My life for the sheep." The devil has sinned (violated the divine law) from the beginning." Jesus was made manifest to undo the works of the devil. Jesus said, "my love shall not depart from you." **(James chapter 1: 13)** "Let no man say he is tempted or tried by God." **(James 1: 17)** "Every *good* gift is from above. (**Isaiah 53: 4**) "Surely He has borne our griefs . . ." (**1 Corinthians 15.: 26**) The *last* enemy is death.

If disease is God's will why aren't we happy about it? Why spend so much money on medical bills? (**Hebrews. 2: 14**) He (Jesus) might bring to naught him who has the power of death-the devil.

If we *believe in our heart that God raised Jesus from the dead, and confess with our mouth that Jesus is our Lord, we become a Christian.* We will go to heaven *(Romans 10: 8-13)*

We believe that when we die, our spirits go directly to be with God in heaven; that we will be resurrected and (receive a new physical body someday.) It's explained in the Bible (**Romans chapter ten starting at verse eight.**) There's more about it in (**II Corinthians chapter 5: verse 8**).

The Bible is made up of 66 different books, most of them by different authors, inspired by God. Even though some of the Old Testament books were written thousands of years ago with hundreds of years between many of the writings, every book in the Old Testament (written before the birth of Jesus), points to Him. Everything that was prophesied about Him, in the Old Testament, He fulfilled to the letter during His time here on earth. Everything you ever heard or read about Jesus was prophesied in the Old Testament. It gives his exact birthplace, (Bethlehem) (**Micah 5:2**) that He would have a star, (**Numbers 24: 17**). Ancient Babylonian clay tablets, now in the British museum in London, confirm that in 7 BCE, Jupiter, known as the star of the Supreme God; Saturn, known as the earthly representative of Jupiter; and Mars, known as the star of Palestine, all converged within the constellation Pisces, known as the constellation of the last days, representing wisdom, life and creation. Jupiter and Saturn changed their normal direction and traveled westward, stopping on November 7th and 20th respectively.

While in Egypt, it is believed the Holy Family stayed in a little town called Materia 6 miles from Cairo where Queen Cleopatra employed a colony of Jewish farmers to tend her grove of Balsam Fir (what we use for Christmas trees) which was planted in 30 BC. (**Isaiah 7: 14**) said the Messiah would be born of a virgin, crucified, (**Isaiah 53: 12**) and what He said while hanging on the cross, (**Psalm 22: 1**). It even predicted His resurrection, (**Psalm 16, verse 10**).

I have mentioned these things to show you why the Bible is the authority for what is in this book, and why it has credibility, and why we can depend on it to be trustworthy down through the generations. It's stood the test of time, truth and reliability. Imagine a gigantic picture puzzle of Biblical history. Some of the pieces have not been found yet to confirm what the Bible has stated, but archaeology *has confirmed* over and over again, that *everything* the Bible says, is exactly true, in every respect!

We must be very careful not to gossip or criticize others, because we could wind up with, or have, the same fault. There's an old saying, "our actions speak so loud, they can't hear what we say."

The Bible has a lot to say about the words we speak. Check out the whole message from the following Scriptures then try and think of another way of expressing your frustration when you are uncomfortable.

We don't appreciate how many others are watching and listening to what we do and say, day by day. (**Proverbs 21: 23**) declares that "He who guards his mouth keeps himself from trouble." (**Proverbs 13: 3**) says that "he who guards his mouth keeps his life." Jesus tells us (**Matthew 12: 34-37**) that each of us will give an account of *every idle, inappropriate word we speak*. He goes on to say that "by our words we will be justified." Ponder this one: "Death and life are in the power of the tongue." (**Proverbs 18: 21.**) And this, in (**Proverbs 11: 13-14**) "The wicked (person) is dangerously snared by the transgression of his lips. In (**James 3**) it tells us of all the destruction our tongue can cause.

The Holy Spirit resides in every Christian and He won't allow any evil spirit to possess them. *A Christian, by exerting his or her own free will,* **can allow the evil spirit to influence him or her. (Hebrews 6: 4-6 & 10: 23-36)** Many people believe that because no one can take their salvation from them that they cannot lose it. These two passages in Hebrews tell us plainly that we can fling it (our salvation) away ourselves!

**How Much Power Does The Devil Really Have?** Military personnel know better than anyone how important it is to understand all the strengths and weaknesses of the enemy. Obviously they don't broadcast them, neither do they ignore them. They try to understand them and plan an effective strategy for victory. The same thing applies to us when dealing with Satan. The less we understand about him the harder he can broadside us when we least expect it.

In the Bible, (**Mark 4: 17**), it talks about persecution on account of God's Word. You will be wise to take a few minutes and see all the ways the devil can get at us. What most of us fail to recognize is, that most of the time we actually allow these things to happen to us by our own actions. The further we allow ourselves to be from God, the more the devil can hurt us!

(**Mark chapter 5**) talks about a man who was totally under the power of demons. They gave him super strength and controlled his mind. Jesus had authority over them. (**Mark 9: 26**) tells about a young man that had seizures. Jesus had power over the seizures also. (**Mark 9: 14**) (**Luke 12: 5**) The Bible tells us that Satan can masquerade as an angel of light to deceive us.

(**II Corinthians 11: 12-15**). Heed the word of the prophet. (**Isaiah in the 5th chapter verses 18-24**) We give the devil power over us when we sin; when we call evil good and good evil; when we put darkness for light and light for darkness; who put bitter for sweet and sweet for bitter and when we are "wise in our own eyes." We need to draw closer to Jesus!

**Reincarnation.** Some people are still confused as to whether or not we die and come back as another person or some animal. Different religions may believe we do. We occasionally hear someone say something like, "In my next life . . . ." Here are some passages in the Bible that tell us that's not the case at all.

Lazarus. In Luke 16: 19, Jesus explains Hades, (hell), prior to His resurrection. In Hades, people had understanding, feelings, and with our sin by suffering emotions. After His crucifixion, Jesus descended into hell, (**Psalm 68: 18**) led a train of vanquished foes and ascended on high, taking them with Him. (**Ephesians 4: 8-12**)

For Christians, to be absent from this body is to be present with the Lord.(**II Corinthians 5: 8-10.** & **I Corinthians 15: 35-58**) goes into great detail about our resurrected bodies going to be with God in heaven. Job says in (**Job 19:26**) "In my flesh I *see* God." There is an interesting scripture: (**Daniel 12: 13**) an angel tells Daniel that he would stand in his "allotted place" at the end of the days. In (**Hebrews**

**chapter 11 and 12)** the Bible talks about the great cloud of witnesses, Christians who have died and are watching us, as if they are in the bleachers at a sports stadium. **(Hebrews 13: 17)** Jesus said that we all must render an account of ourselves (after we die). In the end times a child will safely play with poisonous snakes. The righteous will shine like the sun. A wolf and a lamb will dwell together and the leopard shall lie down in peace with the kid (young goat). **(Isaiah 11: 6)** There are some scriptural references in chapter 3 in this book about animals, that you might want to review.

**Jesus' Defeat of Satan:** Jesus became sin for us, **(II Corinthians 5: 21)** and went into hell to pay for our sins **(John 12: 31-32)** While there, He disarmed principalities **(Colossians 2: 14) Jesus delivered mankind from the haunting fear of death (Ephesians 4: 8).** When God created Adam He gave him *dominion* over the earth and everything in it. Adam gave that dominion to Satan **(Luke 4: 6-7).** Jesus won all of that authority back when He went into hell **(Acts 2: 23-31 and I Corinthians 15: 27). Jesus** gave it back to us before returning to heaven following His resurrection.**(Mark 16: 15-16 & Matthew 28: 16)** In many parts of the world witches, wickens and others that give themselves over to evil exert power and influence over large numbers of people. They use *fear and magic* to gain control. Ungodly religious leaders in our own country exert power over people too. They are very subtle about it. Anything a leader says that does not line up with what the Bible says is a deception.

Put on the full armor that God supplies. **(Ephesians 6: 11-17)** That of a fully armed Roman soldier. The belt of truth, the shield of faith to deflect all the flaming arrows of the evil one, the breastplate of righteousness, the helmet of salvation and boots fitted to spread the Good News of the Gospel of Jesus Christ. We are to take up the **sword of**

**the spirit, which is the Word of God. The Bible tells us that If we reject Jesus as God's son, we reject God.** *(I John 2: 23)* Christians have "all authority over demonic spirits" **(Mark 16: 15-18).**

If you think you are hearing from God and you don't know if it's God or a demon speaking to you, remember, everything must line up (be true) with the Bible. It must <u>not</u> be sinful. I know a guy who said "God told me to divorce my wife and marry another woman." ***NO!*** That does not line up with the Bible! Also, everything must focus on Jesus, <u>not</u> some other spirit or doctrine.

If you are in doubt, ask God to confirm it in the Bible in <u>*two*</u> places. He will. If you wake up in the middle of the night, or at any other time and something frightens you, say, **"in the name of Jesus, leave! Get out of here!"** Drive whatever it is you are fearful of away. If it's demonic, it has to obey a Christian using the name of Jesus! ***Anything from God is not scary.*** If you have any questions go to someone you know to be a Christian for help. Two Christians are better. Ask them to pray with you, and about the situation.

**\*\*\*Commit to having someone you trust with you when you do grief recovery work, individually or in a group. You have a witness to what you say, and your intent and motivation is not going to be misrepresented.**

**Why talk about healing in a grief recovery book?** Anyone trying to cope with a serious illness for themselves or a loved one is not only grieving, but (secretly?) praying for healing! This may be the first time they have thought seriously about God or eternity. No one can throw you a theological curve ball after you understand this material. It just may be, that once someone recognizes the root cause of their problem, they may surrender to God and begin the healing process.

What about "faith healing", "laying on of hands" and "praying over the sick"? **JESUS CHRIST STILL CHANGES LIVES! MIRACLES STILL HAPPEN!** People may be disillusioned by the hypocrisy in many churches today and want to refresh their minds regarding the truth of certain issues. **(Isaiah 5: 20-25.)** The Biblical references are included above to help you, and them. Contact me any time. **pointtheway@myfairpoint.net**

*What about séances, Mediums. talking to the dead, etc?*

Clever Mediums, Wizards, Necromancers etc. are able to snooker many people. They rely on evil spirits to inform them of situations out of the past. The mediums and others give themselves over to these spirits that have been around since day one and know all about peoples' dead relatives. Throughout the Old Testament God commanded His people to actually **kill** anyone doing those things. The Bible says God makes fools of diviners **(Isaiah 44: 25). IT'S ALL EVIL. STAY AWAY FROM IT!**

The only time mediums were recorded to actually have been able to call up the dead is in **I Samuel chapter 28.** King Saul deliberately disobeyed God and later paid for it with his life and the lives of his three sons. Saul was seeking guidance from God, regarding a battle and God had shut him off. Saul wanted the prophet Samuel called up from the dead to advise him. Something happened in the supernatural, because the medium actually saw Samuel. When she did, it terrified her, because the Bible tells us she screamed. Read the account of this in the Bible **(1 Samuel 28)**.

You will almost certainly have people in your grief recovery support groups who have been to fortune tellers, palm readers, tea leaf readers etc. They are all **FAKE**. They somehow are able to communicate with demons, who have been around since day one, and of course they know where your grandmother hid her diamond ring, and a lot of other stuff. This gives the fortune tellers a lot of **power, (AND MONEY).**

**The spirit world.** Most of us don't have a clue about what's going on in the spirit world and wind up being deceived by the devil. I once had a minister that did not believe there was an actual devil. It was ironic. A day or two after it was revealed she believed that way, huge headlines in the daily paper declared that one of the city's police officers was a Satan worshipper. God has a great sense of humor! *The devil certainly is real and can disguise himself as an angel of light. (II Corinthians 11: 12-15)* Sadly many people in one very prominent denomination have been deceived by him.

I know of a number of TV Evangelists that would gladly fight you to the death, arguing that it's *ALWAYS* God's will for a person to be healed. It's just that, as we saw in chapter one, the road of life is filled with potholes that can prevent healing. There are also many other factors that only God knows about. Sin is one of them, generational curses another. These can also prevent prayer from being answered!

**My wife and I had four sons.** Ten years later we unexpectedly had a daughter. She was an affectionate, sweet-natured child, until about twelve or thirteen. Then, she slammed an invisible barrier down between us that I could not penetrate. Overnight she became the typical "strong willed child". Talk about grieving! I was doing it, ***BIG TIME!*** One day as I was talking about her to a friend of mine, a lay preacher. He said to me, "In your mind's eye, picture your daughter standing in front of you. Picture yourself placing your arm around her." I did. "Now, picture Jesus, coming out of the tomb on Easter Sunday morning in all his Glory." I could do that. "Now," he said, "Take your daughter over and give her to Jesus." I *lost it*!

From that day on my fears for her were gone. She was in the care of The Lord and my soul was at rest.

When someone is dealing with a relationship or other difficult issue, the only thing that may help, is to have them give it to Jesus—just as I gave my daughter to Him. He's promised to carry all our burdens cares ***and grief.*** In your mind's eye picture yourself doing this with your loved one.

**All of this material about God,** the devil, evil spirits and heaven is foolishness, if a person does not believe that God is really there and hears our prayers. **Psalm 139** in the Bible says "There is not a word on my tongue (still unuttered) but behold O Lord, You know it altogether." The Psalm tells us that God knit us together in our mother's womb.

When we realize the miracles that take place when a child is born it boggles the mind. The child begins to breath. We didn't breath in our mother's womb. Our lungs did not function. Our whole circulatory system changes. Before birth, everything was supplied by our mother through our umbilical cord. Our digestive system begins to function. We did not digest food, or eat before our birth. We couldn't see. All of these things are not just a coincidence. It's hard work for anyone not to believe there is a God. The evidence of HIS being is overwhelming! Ponder the complexity of the eye, or the ear, or our brain. In the Bible, (**Job, chapter 35)** you will find some of the most beautiful and revealing scripture regarding God's glory and majesty. The Abrahamic Covenant (**Genesis 15)** says. "If you love ME (God) I will bless you. **(I John 5: 18-21)** The evil one touches him not. (The Christian). (**I John 4: 1-4)** Greater is He (The Holy Spirit) that is in me (the Christian), than he that is in the world (the devil).

We are all born with the knowledge of good and evil **(Adam and Eve in the Bible). For someone to say they did not know the difference is a lie.** Fallen angels (demons) want to control people and some people willingly allow them to take over their souls. God gave us a free will. We can allow the Holy Spirit or a demonic spirit to control or enter into us.

**The book is based totally on the Bible with scriptural references.** I believe that in it's original writing the scriptures are true to the letter! I believe every bit of it, not just some of it here and there. Jesus said He had come to fulfill every dotted "i" and crossed "t" written about Him. Many of the original words especially in the Hebrew language had several meanings. For example, our conception of Jesus hanging on the cross is to picture nails driven through the palms of His hands. Actually the word "hands" in the original manuscripts can mean anything from the tips of the fingers to the elbow. Very large nails, nearly the size of railroad spikes were actually driven through the victim's *wrists*. A nail just wouldn't hold a man.

These slight differences do not take away any of the original truth of the Bible. We are as helpless as babes in the woods, and totally ineffective if we do not have LOVE. God does not demand that we love Him or others, but His laws just won't work for us, unless we really do love others, *all* others! That means we cannot harbor unforgiveness in our hearts toward anyone. God cannot prevent the devil from raising havoc with us if we do! Here are some love passages in the Bible. **(I Corinthians chapter 13 & Galatians 6: 1-6. I Corinthians chapters 12, 13 and 14)** We should not think more highly of ourselves than others.

Review chapter one in the book regarding potholes. If we get stuck in one of them it can prevent God from working in us, or through us. Fortunately, God often moves, in spite of the potholes we get ourselves stuck in and blesses us anyway. **Philippians Chapter Four** tells us to always say something good about everybody. There's a story about the funeral of a small town reprobate. The minister asked if somebody would say something good about the man. Nobody spoke. Finally the minister raised his voice and said, "*Can't anybody say something good about this man?*" After a long pause, an old guy in the back of the church stood up and drawled ... "Well, his brother wuz worse!" We need to love the unlovely and place a strong guard on our tongue. Ben Franklin said it best. "There is so much good in the worst of us, and so much bad in the best of us; that it hardly behooves any of us, to talk about the rest of us."

**Healing:** Why have I spent so much time on spiritual warfare and Scriptures? It is because, as soon as we are confronted with a serious illness, or situation for ourselves, or a loved one, we grieve! We also need healing—physical healing and spiritual healing too. Our understanding of the Scriptures and ability to recognize Satan's evil nature will give us and those we want to help a huge advantage. I want you to offer hope and love in the name of Jesus Christ.

**Getting your grief recovery support group up and running:** I'll say it once again. People may not understand that God is not behind death, disease and disaster. The devil raises havoc and then tries to get people to think God did it.

The grief recovery process is long and tedious. **Keep in mind that if someone has an issue that's "bugging" them, something they need to talk about, get off their chest, let them speak. IF ANYONE IS DEALING WITH A PERSONAL SITUATION, AND YOU DON'T DEAL**

## WITH THAT SOON, THE PERSON WILL NOT BE "TUNED IN" TO ANYTHING YOU YOURSELF WANT TO TALK ABOUT.

When you are satisfied that everyone is "tuned in and ready to go to work," begin by asking everyone to tell a little about themselves, and the circumstances surrounding the death of their loved one. If it's a different grief issue, like divorce, a family situation, or being unable to cope with a particular situation, ask the grieving person to describe what's going on. Before your meeting, review chapter two, "Understanding Grief". Encourage everyone to get involved and contribute to the discussion. I've found that others in groups I have facilitated can contribute much more wisdom and advice than I can in particular situations. I believe God places these people in your groups specifically to help others who are hurting. Listen for remarks like, "God took my loved one." "I'm mad at God! I always thought He was a loving God. Why did He let this awful thing happen to my loved one? He was a good person. Hundreds of people were praying for him or her. Why didn't God answer our prayers?" You may want to go back and review the first of the chapter.

With these kinds of questions it's clear the grieving person does not understand about Satan. At the first meeting I ask everyone of the people there to read the first chapter of the book of Job in the Bible, as a homework assignment. Then we spend as much time as we need to going over it, so there is no question in anyone's mind that Satan is behind disasters and death. Not God.

Next, I suggest you review the first part of this chapter that explains why God didn't do it. Then go over each one of the scriptures with your group. Take the time to have different ones read the scripture passages so what you are trying to get across actually sinks in.

After that, I ask someone to read the 139th Psalm aloud. We discuss just how much God is involved in our lives. This also reinforces the fact that He does no do things to hurt us, or cause illness etc.

Next I would suggest you go through the stages of grief with everyone. Instead of identifying the feelings as "stages", ask everyone to comment about each one separately, like shock, at learning about the death or problem. Talk about everyone's feelings of denial. Ask if anyone felt bewildered, in a daze. How long did that phase of the grieving process last? Did they wonder if they might be "losing it?" How did they get through that situation? Did they have support by their family or friends? What kind of support? Within a few weeks I would ask someone to read the 91st Psalm for everyone, and also the sixth chapter of Ephesians verse 12, through to the end of the chapter, out loud.

I would go into the "pothole" section of chapter one, and be sure everyone has an opportunity to express themselves about each one of them. Ask each one if they had gotten "stuck" in any of them, or if they know anyone who had been stuck in one of them. Stress forgiveness, because without it there is no healing! Follow the outline and don't skip anyone when it comes to discussing each topic; you may want to skip around, but sooner or later, come back to each one, for the sake of everybody. **I don't know if I'll see my spouse, (family member or friend) in heaven** is something I often hear from people in my groups. Only God knows for sure. However over the years I have talked with many people who didn't know they were going to die soon. Usually they asked a lot of questions about spiritual things that they were not interested in before.

I believe God places a desire to know Him on peoples' hearts before they die. I believe He gives everyone the opportunity of accepting or rejecting Him. Many people who I believed were not going to make it into heaven came to a saving knowledge of Christ, lying on their death bed or shortly before. It may be that people who suffer a long time with some disease like cancer, are given that additional time to make a commitment to Jesus before they die, so I would never say a loved one is not in heaven. One of the most powerful ads I have ever seen was a picture of several people in a clothes closet with a huge coat hanger across their shoulders so they appeared to be hanging there in the closet. The caption under the picture read, "Are you a closet Christian?"

## Jesus Christ Still Changes Lives! Miracles Still Happen!

**Take all of this VERY seriously!** There is an account in the Bible, **(Acts chapter 19: verse 13)** of men who did not know Jesus and were trying to cast out an evil spirit. The spirit beat them, ripped their clothes off and sent them fleeing in terror!

There is power in the supernatural. Unless you are a Christian, **do not** try and cast out demons, or do anything else using the name of Jesus! If you are a Christian, do not do any of this without another mature Christian with you!

In many situations grieving is the result of deep emotional wounding. Only God can give the person peace. Prior to any support group meeting, pray for wisdom and guidance. Ask for the ability to discern the difference between the need for inner healing and the need to offer (or receive) forgiveness. Pray for an anointing of (by) the Holy Spirit. If you are a

Christian, the Holy Spirit always abides within you and goes with you wherever you go.

If inner healing is needed, ask Jesus to return to the memory of the event that caused the wounding. Ask Him to take the poison, bitterness and resentment out of the memory of the incident. Ask Him to fill you, or the one that has been wounded, with all His love and peace.

If unforgiveness is an issue, ask that He (Jesus) fill you, or the one being prayed for, with all the love and forgiveness that He (Jesus) won on the cross, when He said, "Father, forgive them, for they know not what they are doing." Luke 23: 34

If you are in need of forgiveness, ask God to forgive you. If you need to forgive another person, seek him or her out and ask for it. If they have died, or moved, picture the person in your mind's eye, and verbally ask for their forgiveness. Then ask God to forgive you. If you are helping someone who has not completed their relationship with, or had the opportunity to say their good-byes to the one that has died, ask them to picture the one that has died in their mind's eye.

Say to the person, "ARE THERE THINGS YOU WISH YOU COULD HAVE SAID TO YOUR LOVED ONE THAT YOU DIDN'T GET A CHANCE TO SAY TO THEM BEFORE THEY DIED?"

Say to them, "PICTURE THAT PERSON IN YOUR MIND'S EYE NOW **AND SAY WHAT YOU NEED TO *SAY TO THAT PERSON.*"** Usually they will say, "I love you." *Ask them,* "*ARE THERE OTHER THINGS BESIDES I LOVE YOU?*"

There are those who think all this is foolishness. In the Bible, in the book of Hebrews, in chapters 11 and 12, it tells us that a great "cloud of witnesses", who are our relatives and friends, are watching and presumably hearing everything we say. No matter what, our message is communicated. We have a guardian angel (**Matthew 18: 10**) and God knows our thoughts before we think them and our words before we even speak them(**Psalm 139**). God **will** give us forgiveness. All we need to do is ask.

### Christianity can be summed up in one word
### Jesus

If you believe in your heart that God raised Jesus
up from the dead,
and confess with your mouth that He (Jesus) is
**your** Lord, you shall be saved.
**When this happens, God will send Hiss Holy
Spirit to live within your heart.
Romans 10: 9. Ephesians 2: 8. John 15.
It is by Grace, you are saved, through your faith.
You can't be good enough, work hard enough, or
buy your way into heaven.**

The Christian will not try and force you to believe this. He or she will just love you. No matter how bad anyone hurts the Christian, they are to forgive them.

Why was Jesus born of a virgin? (God doesn't even require that you believe this.)

It goes back to Adam and Eve and the Garden of Eden. Every one of us inherited Adam's sin nature. We also inherited the knowledge of good and evil. No one has to tell us that it's wrong to kill or steal (The Ten Commandments, **Deuteronomy Chapter 5**). God requires a blood sacrifice for sin. **Genesis 3: 21.** Jesus was the perfect, sinless sacrifice for all of us. To be born sinless He had to be born of God and of a virgin.

May God Bless You

## Section Six

Grief Recovery Support Groups. This program began years ago when I learned that training was available to help widowed persons organize and lead support groups. I had no idea they'd send a trainer to a small town in Maine, but they did. There were enough enthusiastic widows that wanted some kind of a social life, who were interested enough to make the program work. They took the training, formed a governing board from the community at large, and for quite a few years a <u>*very*</u> successful widowed person's social support group flourished.

I moved. The leadership didn't take my advice and after several years the group *imploded*! They became complacent. Strong friendships developed and they became an exclusive "club"(Us four, <u>*no*</u> more). For years I thought they were not reaching out enough to the new widows in the community. The truth is, I was dead wrong. It took me quite a few years to figure out what went wrong and several more to figure out how to develop a comprehensive program that would work. The following is what happened to wake me up.

I was confident I could organize another widowed person's support group in my new area, similar to my first one. I had recently worked with several younger widows that I felt would get along well together and help me organize the new group. I invited about a dozen younger to middle aged widows to an organizational meeting and asked them to bring their widowed friends with them.

I began by talking about my original group; how it was organized and all the social activities they enjoyed. Then I talked about all the fun things these women could do. About half way through my presentation, an intelligent young widow, I had pictured as eventually leading the group, got up in a huff and stormed out of the building, taking about half the other women there with her!

There I was, devastated, standing in the middle of the floor, trying to figure out what I did that I shouldn't have done, or what I had not done, that I should have. It took me *years* to figure out what went wrong that evening. Then it hit me like a ton of bricks. Neither the young widow who stormed out of the room on me that evening, nor any of the others who left with her, were ready for *anything* SOCIAL in their lives at that time. In defense of the original group; they *were* reaching out to the recently widowed, as they had been taught, but they were trying to integrate them into the social program much *too soon*. The recently widowed just didn't "fit" in with the social crowd and their leadership hadn't had enough experience to realize what was happening.

The lesson I learned from that sad experience is: Don't try and rush a grieving person into any group, especially a "social" group. They won't enjoy it and their attitude will adversely affect everyone else around them!

This led me to the conclusion that *two distinct groups were needed*; the socially oriented club-type group, who were finally ready to step out and take their place in the community again, plus a *grief recovery support group* for the more recently widowed. (This group would be trying to cope with the early "stages of grief" we talked about earlier in the book.)

As I facilitated more support groups, it became clear to me that *many* newly widowed women were not yet ready to become part of a grief recovery support group *and probably would not be,* for a considerable length of time, following the death of their husbands.

After facilitating several other groups, I came to realize that a very important element was missing from this new program. That was the *mentoring process* for the recently widowed. A widow (or widower, for that matter) needs time to recoil following the death of their spouse. Often there are a million things that need to be taken care of, RIGHT NOW, YESTERDAY, as soon as services are over. Families have to return to their own daily routine and the widow or widower is left alone with all the details that have to be tended to. I experienced an emotional exhaustion following my first wife's death that only a lot of sleep could cure.

There's no such thing as a "return to normal" for a widowed person. Everything in their life has been turned upside down, overwhelming many. Sometimes their married friends abandon them socially. Everyone is busy. The newly widowed person desperately needs a support system. Women especially are vulnerable to all kinds of people trying to take advantage of them. If there is no family close by, it's worse, they're lonely. Some grieving people want to isolate. On the other side of the coin, I knew one widow that visited every support group for miles around because she just wanted to get out of the house.

A few days following memorial services or funeral, someone from your support group should contact the new widow. It would be just a friendly "hello, Jane"(or whatever her name is.) If the caller hasn't done so privately before, tell her, "I'm in the widowed persons' support group," how are you doing? Need help with anything? Want to get out of the house for a cup of coffee for a few minutes? I'm free. I'll pick you up in ten minutes. Becky from the support group will be with me. Do you know Becky?"

If she would prefer not to go out, set up a comfortable time for a visit. I sense there are some red flags that just unfurled, because no widow in her right mind would accept an appointment with a stranger.

As your group becomes better known and people in the community become familiar with your goals and objectives, your credibility will not be questioned. Community leaders will go out of their way to refer grieving people to you. One of the first things you should do is print a tri-fold flier and place copies in every business in the area. Anyone with a computer and printer can produce a pretty good brochure to get you started. Contact your Better Business Bureau, Chamber of Commerce, or merchant's group, right off and invite them to come and speak to your new group.

Everyone in the group, working in teams, will become Ambassadors of Good Will. Use this approach. "This is our flyer. This is what we do. If you know a widow who is grieving, please give one of these to her. We'll invite her to the next support group. We'll be glad to talk with her anytime. Our number is right here."

Be sure the police know about you. Someone in your group will know the Chief. Invite him to come and speak to your group about security, self defense or other issue. Every church should be personally contacted. Pastors should also be invited to refer their people to your group. Stress that your group talks about God. They may want to read the chapter about God in your book. Loan it to them. Certainly each funeral home should know of your group. They may even place your flyers out for their families. A very small ad every day in your daily paper with a contact phone number may get you inquiries. Some businesses that advertise a lot may donate a few inches each week to you. Businesses buy ad space and are probably paying for more than they need to get their message across. Most newspapers have a free public service announcement page. If the daily paper does not offer this service, most areas have monthly papers that are free to the public. (Advertisers pay the cost.) Check out their ad space for a piggyback. Don't forget your public library, professional offices, banks, beauty and barber shops. Public relations and good publicity are the keys.

What if there is already a widowed person's social support group in town? Usually groups like this are pretty tightly controlled. They almost certainly will not want to change. As more and more from your grief recovery support group "graduate" to *their* social organization, and offer suggestions, the better that organization will become. If widows know there is something better, they may want to start a group of their own. You can guide them, but do not initiate change! Other widowed persons' support groups, from what I've heard, are pretty much social clubs, with no agenda, or they are grief recovery programs only. As I mentioned in the last chapter, most facilitators are afraid *not* to be "politically correct" and refuse to allow people to talk about God. By not charging for your program, keeping it very small, and putting your groups together with people *you* know, or by referrals from people who know you, no one can say you can't do what you are doing(as long as we're a free country).

Invite individual widows, or women with other grief related issues, to your grief recovery support groups. Let word of mouth be your advertising. It won't take more than one or two groups for word to spread that your program really is helpful. These women will know if your city will support another social group or not. If there already is one, the best thing to do might be to start small grief recovery groups for the time being. Then, these folks can integrate from your group into the existing social group. Talk with someone who has been in another support group, and tell them what this one has to offer. Loan them this book. Every situation is different. (You might want to pray about it). As long as I am able, I will offer suggestions if you want to contact me.

**Here is where the mentoring process begins**. It's the third and I believe most critical facet in a widow's complete recovery. It's where *two* widows, who have worked through their own grief and truly understand how a new widow is feeling, come alongside her and walk with her, during these first weeks following the death of her mate. Two members from your social group would commit to mentoring her, together, until she's ready to enter a grief recovery support group. They also agree to call her occasionally between visits. The new widow should feel free to call one of the mentors whenever she has a need to talk.

Eventually, as the social group grows, every new widow in the area (with their approval and permission). will have two widows they can call on for help, advice and support whenever they need it. Do not allow a person to mentor more than one new widow at a time! Always have teams of two widows visit the newly widowed person at one time! When the recently widowed woman is ready to enter a grief recovery support group, the two widows who are mentoring her will know it instinctively and see to it that she is is integrated into the next support group that's formed. Facilitators of grief recovery support groups will know when to take that widow to a meeting of the social support group and introduce her to the others.

Another person from your support group should call the new widow from time to time to be sure she is doing well with the mentors. If there is any problem, personality-wise or otherwise, the mentor(s) should be replaced I've talked with many widows over the years who have told me that just having someone who would sit with them and listen, to have a cup of coffee with them or to answer their questions had helped them immensely over the roughest bumps on their grief journey. This new widowed person's support program assures that this is not overlooked.

If for some reason, the widow is not interested in the mentoring program, don't force the issue. Have someone from your social group board of directors call her about once a month. After several months, invite her to join a grief recovery support group. She may have some friend, or relative who is providing mentoring for her. She might just be a very private person. Anyway, she will know you are interested in her, and after several months she might just give the grief recovery support group a try.

You remember that grief recovery support groups are five or six people max. The widow works with *two* mentors for a few weeks before integrating into a grief recovery support group. Both she and her mentors will know when the time is right for her to do that. My experience has been that it will be at least six months from the time she enters the grief recovery support group until she is ready to "graduate" to the social group.

A facilitator with an assistant can start a gri*ef recovery support* group with as few as two or three widows. If another woman is dealing with a pressing grief issue, like teenage rebellion, divorce, miscarriage, a serious medical problem or death of a sibling, welcome her into the group. These are all grief related issues that are talked about specifically in chapter 2 and 3. Ask each woman if they know another one who might also like to be in a support group. Very likely they will. You'll probably have to march in place for a few weeks while the social group leadership lines up a facilitator and an assistant and two or three other widows to start a group. Usually newcomers bond quickly, but there is a time when a new person in the group is no longer welcome. You probably remember, we covered that in detail in chapter 2.

This is how the new grief recovery program works most effectively. All three phases of the program fall under one umbrella. Each phase works independently of each other and complements the others. Everyone is accountable to the board of directors of the social group. This way there is ongoing support within the organization. Obviously, if there is no social group with a board of directors you are only accountable to the Good Lord. It has worked very well for me to facilitate my groups within my church structure. A business, like a funeral home, assumes accountability. Follow these guidelines and there should be no problem. My current E-mail is listed at the end of the chapter. I'll be glad to give you any advice I can.

If another organization, like a church or funeral home, wants to establish their own social support group, there are checks and balances built into the Bi-laws and Board of Directors structure so a certain amount of leadership and control stays with the sponsoring party. Through a church, their nonprofit status and liability will cover the group. My first group was sponsored by the YMCA. They also gave us an office in their building. **Do not incorporate under the IRS code # 5 0 1 c 3.**

If you want to have a grief recovery support group with several people you know, there is no problem having it. You are not doing counseling or therapy and you are not charging. You are merely helping friends over the roughest bump in their lives right now. Later, after these people recognize that you have helped them and are ready to step out again and become part of the community, loan them this book. Everyone in your social group should read it anyway, so they have an understanding of grief; hopefully they too will be able to help friends and family around them.

If there is no social group for widows in your area, and you're interested, or know someone that might be, take a serious look at this material. It's a _comprehensive_ program that will work. It's not difficult. As a matter of fact it's fun. My intention, when I started writing this book was to offer a resource to small group leaders of production teams in the business environment, or Bible study groups at churches, etc. I could visualize fire and police departments integrating this material into their support group programs. Although I have never facilitated a veteran's support group, the material seems perfect to add too any existing program. In those types of situations, that's as far as the recovery would go, unless a grief recovery group wanted to become a long term social group.

Organizing the social group is included here specifically for a widowed persons' program, but it certainly could be adapted to many other situations. It shows you how to organizing a group and set up an *ideal board of directors*. There are also suggestions for some worthwhile projects to get started with. Encourage members to come up with projects they would like to participate in and present at board meetings Loan this book to the leadership of any organization that might be interested in sponsoring you. This is not as complicated as it seems right now. Here are a few suggestions for starting a

Widowed Persons' Social Support Group in your area. Talk with two or three women who have been widowed more than a year. They will *probably* have pretty much resolved their personal grief issues and can look back objectively. Organize a social group first if there is none. It's not complicated, but you will need to make a time and emotional commitment.

If you don't know enough women who have been widowed more than a year, start a grief recovery support group with two or three who have been more recently widowed. When they are ready to move on, ask them to invite their friends that have been widowed awhile and start a social group. Many women are uncomfortable going anywhere alone, socially. The prospect of having a group of mature, single women to have fun with, is very appealing.

**Widowers groups** are *very* hard to get going. I strongly recommend you wait until you've had experience with a grief recovery support group for widows before doing anything with men. The best way to get a widower any kind of support, beyond what you yourself are now capable of offering, is to try to get him involved in a men's group at an area church. Then see if they will allow you to train the group in grief recovery principles. You have the ability to empower many people in different walks of life.

*Do not mix men and women, either in small grief recovery groups or larger social groups.* Most older men are terrified at the thought of a bunch of "old hens" pecking at them. After you get your social group up and running, go ahead and have an old fashioned "box social".

Caution: If you are a man, have your spouse or someone you trust with you at all your group meetings. You have a witness for anything you say, and no one has an opportunity to accuse you of anything improper. A man can facilitate a women's group, with a co-facilitator(man or woman) but it's doubtful that a woman would have much success with a grief recovery group of all men. Be sure all elderly and handicapped widows are plugged into your "system". Stay alert. The spouse of the widowed person may have been the one that gave them their meds and managed household finances. There may be some _real_ needs there. Your team from the social group may very well be the only ones available (or able) to help. It will take time to develop trust. Be sure there is a follow-up from the board of directors in every situation where this type of dependency can develop! Don't hesitate to seek legal counsel where finances are involved.

## Some Reasons Small Groups Are Not Successful

1. The Facilitator doesn't "engage" emotionally. Small group meetings can be very intense! If the facilitator isn't completely "with it" the participants won't be either and the facilitator will be branded a phony. He or she must be willing to totally engage with everyone, cry with them, empathize.
2. The Environment isn't "Right". Too hot, too cold, too many distractions, too many people, chairs not comfortable, may not like others in group, etc.
3. Too Structured. Many small group meetings have a specific format and the facilitator isn't willing to bend; to allow participants to find their familiarity level. Often the facilitator's attitude is, "This is what has to be done and _this_ is how _I'm_ doing it, so let's get this show on the road and get it over with ASAP."
4. Not Enough Time. The moment people in a group feel "pressured" for time you've lost them! Everyone must feel completely relaxed and know they can talk about what _they_ want to talk about, when _they_ want

to talk about it! It may seem like some meetings are just meandering along. That's OK. *When they* feel comfortable with each other *and* you, they'll get down to serious business, *not* before. I spent about two hours one afternoon during a grief recovery session, while *everyone* just fooled around. They laughed and they told jokes. Everyone was in a partying mood. Then, without a thing being said, the atmosphere changed completely. Those women accomplished more in ten minutes than we usually did in an entire afternoon. Our weekly meetings were averaging about two and a half hours.

People have told me that in some support groups everyone is allowed just so much time to speak and they have to speak in turn. No interaction is allowed. Most support groups are on a strict time schedule. "Time's up, It's over, see 'ya next week, good bye!"

5. Facilitator Doesn't Understand Small Group Dynamics. There's an art to letting people interact with you and each other. It's a greater art to get them to open up. and share their innermost feelings with other people. I saw some grief recovery support groups develop into close knit *fellowship* groups that lasted for years. When you sense you have completed the grief recovery process with a group, back out gradually. Some in the group may want to continue on as a social club.

## Let 'Em Go

Some people seem to want to dominate every conversation. Be patient. If someone has something "eating at them," you probably won't get anything done in your group until this person gets whatever it is that's bugging them off their chest. There are many reasons why some people want to dominate.

One is because no one else will listen to them. They _know_ they're being selfish. You don't have to remind them.

Be patient and be gentle. Sooner or later the person will wind down. If the person gets out of hand, ask them privately to _help you_ with whatever the problem seems to be. This person could become *the best workhorse in the organization.* Try to find out what's beneath the anxiety. Become their "special friend." Don't forget, some people have _years_ of pent up emotions that need to be let out, neediness that needs to be healed.

I remember one mild mannered woman who didn't say a whole lot, usually. One evening something was said that triggered her emotions and she let loose. She'd had a hard life and her teenage daughter had recently died. For most of the meeting she just let it all out—years of grief and suppressed emotions, tears, frustration, anger, all of it. She just went on and on. Everybody else just let her go. She was fine after that. But she needed to get rid of that load of grief. You can expect that type of outburst at any time. Just have the tissues and cold water handy.

Arrange for transportation for women living in isolated or high crime areas. Many will not go out at night, period. In that case, have meetings during daylight. hours. I wouldn't try to have more than one grief recovery support group going at one time to start with. It's emotionally draining.

Within a couple of years you'll have several "teams" that can operate without your direct week to week involvement. However, if you are operating through a church, funeral home, or any sponsoring organization you _will_ be able to maintain a certain amount of influence and leadership, just by the way the board is set up. So pay strict attention to the details and structure of the original board and By-laws.

Continue to be a mentor and maintain personal contact with everyone. Have women facilitators work with widows and male facilitators with widowers. Never mix the two groups, except for social occasions.

Here's some suggestions for a recruitment letter to a woman widowed about a year or more. You can use it for a woman who has lost a significant other or modified for widowers.

> Dear Mrs. (Ms.)
>
> You are invited to become a member of a new <u>*non*</u> <u>political</u> support organization for widows being formed in our community.
>
> A widowed person's support group gives women who have <u>*somewhat*</u> recovered from their grief over a period of months, (and only when they are ready) an opportunity to come together for support, companionship, service and social activities. Groups usually meet on a monthly (sometimes weekly) basis and become involved in community service, as facilitators for grief recovery support groups, volunteerism and a new mentoring program for the recently widowed.
>
> Part of our long range plan is to ask members from the socially oriented group to reach out and mentor women who have *recently been widowed*.
>
> I'd really appreciate your advice and help during the early planning stages for this Group. Please share with me what kinds of things you and any widowed friends of yours

might be interested in doing *right <u>now</u>*. Also if you (or any one of them) would be willing to serve on an organizational committee to help make those things happen, it would be greatly appreciated.

Please fill in the survey at your earliest convenience and drop it in the mail. Call me if you have any questions, or just want to talk about it. We will be having our first organizational meeting depending on the results of our survey. Signed _____

**If several of your friends are planning to start the group with you, have them sign the letter, too.**

PS: If you know any widow who might be interested in this type of group, please talk with her, obtain her mailing address and let me know, so I can send her a survey. We are also planning to introduce grief recovery support groups for widows who are not ready for social activities: women who can arrange to meet weekly for help and encouragement. This is not "counseling" or "therapy." Just common sense, every day, down to earth "stuff" that brings results. It's also For those who have worked through their grief issues and would like to empower others to reach out. It is absolutely FREE.

## Survey Regarding A Widowed Person's Social Support Group

(For women widowed a year or more and ready to move on with their lives)

* Have you had experience working with *any* support group of any kind?
* Would you like to meet with other widowed women? Yes _____ No _____.
* If speakers were available, which of the following topics would you be interested in?
  Home security? _____ Personal Safety? _____ Insurance _____? Health issues _____? Financial issues? _____ Health issues? _____
* If you have other suggestions, please share them. Write on the back of this page.
* I need someone *right now*, to talk with me personally (or members of my family) and help me work through my (their) grief. _____.

We are also forming a small grief recovery support group at this time. Would you be interested in becoming one of the group? Please call me (us) if you are.

* Others in my family need help working through their grief. _____
* I'm ready to get out a little with other widowed persons. _____
* What would you enjoy doing with others in a support group? Volunteering at a Nursing Home _____. Visiting shut-ins _____ Crafts _____ Working with elderly _____ kids _____ Sewing _____. Knitting _____. Playing cards _____. Community activities _____ (non political). Physical activity like hiking _____ Swimming _____?
* I'm ready to help others who have been more recently widowed. _____
* I'd like to be in a grief recovery support group with a few others. _____
* I'd like to become involved in the planning process for a support group. _____
* I'd prefer a Breakfast meeting _____ Luncheon meeting _____ Evening meeting. _____ Mid-morning meeting. _____ Mi-afternoon meeting. _____
* Is there a day of the week that is best for you. What's your second preference?
* Would you be willing to car pool? Yes _____ No _____
* Do you have a car? Yes _____ No _____
* If Yes, would you be willing to drive others? Yes _____ No _____
* Would you need transportation to the meeting? Yes _____ No _____.

I would appreciate any comments you'd like to make.

Please use other side of paper for comments

## Bi-laws & Organizational Tips

This is a great blueprint for any governing body small business, non-profit, setting up a corporation. Appoint a _small_ Bi-Laws committee. (3 to 5). Don't set any deadline. Borrow the best ideas from other groups in area. You'll be amazed at how much savvy a group has. Don't expect a lawyer to donate legal services for you to incorporate. (They'll tell you it's not allowed by state law.) Be _sure_ Bi-laws state that the group must reach out to the newly widowed! Another "must" to have in them is that every project and every activity _must_ be voted on and passed by a unanimous vote of the board of directors! (_Warning_ If you don't, two or three well meaning members will likely go off by themselves and plan projects that may not be good for the organization as a whole. (Don't take this lightly; I've seen it happen with other groups.) Allow board members to cast absentee votes, or vote by phone. (Be sure and document!) Hand pick your first Board of Directors! Limit the board to _officers_. (Spelled out later). Don't exclude widows who have re-married from membership in your support group. They are a _terrific resource_ for the newly widowed. Get everyone's opinions on all group business, pro and con.

Caution: believe it or not, there are those who would infiltrate your group. People who are anti-funeral, anti-memorialization, even anti-Christian, if your new group is church oriented. If the sponsoring organization is a business, be sure no competitor, or competitor-friendly person, is invited to sit on your initial board. This is why it is so critical that you hand pick your first board of directors.

With my first widowed persons' support group, we invited the community-at-large to help us organize and establish a board of directors. Wouldn't you know it, one of the original board members was anti-funeral! This woman was a thorn in my side from the get-go.

Why is this such a big deal? Because, for most widows, sentiment, memorialization and the concept of family and community coming together for support and love at the time of death is extremely important. Some anti-funeral people do not share Jewish or Christian values, nor the other concepts I just mentioned. However, the Bible has references to burial, grieving, and even embalming, dating back in Jewish history to Abraham, Moses, Jacob and Joseph. **Genesis chapter 50. Deuteronomy 34: 7 and 8. Acts 7: 15-16.** Be warned.

**You're off and running!** Be at *every* board meeting as a non-voting "advisor" as much as possible (after the first year). This will assure that no one from the outside dominates the agenda, or changes the structure and purpose of the group. Insist that board meetings are open for any member to sit in on, but not vote. Plan one key project like a holiday memorial service, a town improvement project or something similar that the group can do together, *right off*. Your Bi-laws should not allow board members (officers), to chair any committee. You want to get as many different members involved as possible. You may want to require that chairmen of committees or their representative attend all board meetings so questions can be answered on the spot. Rules like this should be written into the Bi-laws.

*Governing Body*: Your *most* effective board will have five members. The first year, you, the organizer sits on the board in the place of Past President with one vote. Each year the immediate Past President stays on the board as a voting advisor. You, the organizer, will be a non-voting advisor, (*not a voting board member*), from then on. You'll be able to see the leadership potential when you organize, so hand pick your President, Secretary, Treasurer and Activities Director very carefully. For the first year, you, the organizer, are the tie-breaking vote, if necessary. After that, the Activities Director becomes the President. The Treasurer becomes the Activities Director. The Secretary becomes the Treasurer and the new member on the board becomes Secretary. As I said before, the President stays on as voting Advisor. The next year she's off the board. _You, the organizer,_ continue year after year as non-voting advisor. A unanimous yes vote should definitely be required to launch each and every new project. Each Chairwoman will want to pick her own committee.

The Activities Director is automatically on every committee and should attend most committee meetings. She represents the board and speaks for them. She will work hand in hand with the Chairman. If several members bring a project before the board, let them choose their own chair. She also assumes the role of publicity director.

## Here are some Tips For A Great Publicity Release

1. Get to know the local reporter if there is one and feed the information to him or her. They usually work on commission of some kind and if they know you can be a source of information now, and later too, you will have made a good friend.
2. Use as many names as possible. Supply them with as many photos as you can.
3. Invite the reporter to a working lunch.
4. Date your article. If possible hand deliver it, and ask for suggestions and help.
5. Identify yourself (or publicity director) and how to get in contact with you.
6. Use large enough font for easily reading (12 or 14). Double space. One side of paper only.
   Leave wide margins so notes may be easily added.

7. Submit *only* *one* story at a time. However submit several articles about the same project.
   Just before your big event, do a complete story about the project, using all the names and
   (a.) Headline: Support Group Plans Fund Raiser for (specific charity)
   (b.) Another headline next week. Jane Pickering, Chairman of Green Valley Widowed Person's Group Names Sally Longfellow Chairman of Fundraising for (specific charity).
   (c.) (Next week.) Sally Longfellow, Chairman of Fundraising for (specific charity) names Committee.
   (d.) Fund Raising Activities for (specific charity) Announced By Sally Longfellow: (for example). 1. Fruit Sale. 2. Charity Ball. 3. Walk-A-Thon, 4. Talent Show. (etc.)
   (e.) An article about each of the fund raisers and all people involved.
   (f.) New information on each event. Example: Info re: fruit sale. What's involved. Where to place orders. Place of distsribution. Photo of fruit being delivered. Committee at work. Announcements about talent show, each contestant. Support staff. If your reporter is really good he, or she will get a headline for the actual event and a recap of the project.
   (g.) Be sure and have a follow-up of amount raised, a statement by the leader of the recipient group, and what the funds (or purchase) will actually be used for. At the end of each article put in a tiny blip about your organization. For example Green Valley Widowed Person's Club is a nonprofit organization meeting at \_\_\_\_\_ on the first & third Friday each month at 9:00 AM. Include a quick re-cap of information

from previous articles. Always say ... For more information call (123) 456-7890.

Again, briefly, any activity your group does is news. If it involves people, use their names. Break everything down into sections and tell everything about that part of the project. Type your information out neatly. Headline it, leave wide margins, double space and date. Hand deliver if possible, so you maintain personal contact. Always include the contact person's name, phone number (or Email).

Newspapers need local stories to sell copies. They know that if people are going to have their names in the paper, they'll buy the paper and their friends and family will too. This is an excellent way to get to know newspaper staff. It's that type of contact that will convince them to do a feature story on your group.

If there are competing papers, try and release your information so one paper is not able to "scoop" the other one. Weeky or local papers should receive preferential treatment, because they are the ones that will give you better coverage, and a possible feature story. Daily papers probably won't print something that was headlined in the weekly or local paper. The trick is to release the information so it's run in both papers on the same day. Important: If each committee appoints one person to handle publicity for that committee and work with the Activities Director, collect and type the information for the press releases, using the above guidelines, so that no one is going to be over-burdened.

One last thing: if the President has to resign, leaves, or is unable to do her duties, have your Bi-laws state that the Past President that went off the board last, sit in as President for the remainder of the term. When the Past President goes off the board, she shall wait at least one year before going back on the board. This way you do not have the same people dominating the agenda year after year.

*Don't* do this alone—have a trusted friend help you

- A. Find someone with whom you'd like to work in organizing the group.
- B. Send letters. Follow up with phone calls in a few days. Find meeting place, plan refreshments, etc. (absolutely not necessary, but great P/R.)
- C. Get together with all interested widows. Explain the program.
- D. Observe who is "fired up", who might fill leadership roles.
- E. Have everyone invite widowed friends to your next meeting. (They should have been widowed about a year or more.)
- F. When they meet, review and plan next meeting. (Activities, refreshments, goals.)
- G. Sit back and let the widowed persons take the lead. (I/D a leadership team.) Appoint a different separate Bi-laws committee.
- H. Pick your officers. Get newcomers involved. Avoid letting one or two do all the work. Keep a tight rein on finances.
- I. Do not allow (in your Bi-laws) one person to have more than one leadership role, like officer and chairman of a committee at the same time. It would be great if you could get a sponsor for your group. A church would be ideal. Another club like Rotary, or a funeral home, or a bank would work. The YMCA sponsored my first group. They covered us for liability and our board met there.

## Fun Activities for Widowed Persons Social Support Groups

Auctions, Art Shows, Activity each month, Adopt a needy family

* Bake appreciation cookies for the fire dept., police dept., rescue & charities
* Beach party, baby sit for overstressed moms, low income families etc.
* Playing cards with shut-ins, handicapped, elderly, or nursing home patients. (Private card parties can raise finances for charitable groups.)
* Make favors and volunteer at nursing homes.
* Bar-B-Q for veterans, prison inmates' families, street kids, slum areas.
* Invite exchange students and college kids from away to meal, meeting, party.
* Teach crafts to kids, shut-ins, retired groups handicapped, youth centers etc.
* Become companion to shut-ins, handicapped, disabled veterans.
* Craft fair, yard sale outing at a park, swimming pool, beach.
* Run errands for shut-ins and wheel chair bound persons. Housework chores for elderly, one parent households, sickly, overstressed.
* Holiday activities(any holiday.) An enthusiastic committee can come up with lots of ideas.
* Kids projects: Big Brother/Sister, Youth Center, Scouting, "Y"Camp, After School Program.
* Work with law enforcement officials for mentoring programs.
* Organize fun activities for kids. Parties, roller skating, bowling, etc.
* Get involved with community activities like field days, floats, special events, etc.

* Sponsor musical events like an interfaith sing-along, old fashioned community sing-along
* Talent shows, music in the park evenings, street dance, square dance for everyone
* Sponsor, or work with a group having a holiday meal, like Thanksgiving.
  Fun for anyone wanting to be with others at the holiday meal.
* Brighten The Corner Where You Are: Adopt a traffic circle, vacant lot, spruce it up.
* Plantings & welcome signs at entrances to town. Beautification projects everywhere.
* Sponsor breakfast for veterans, fire fighters, police, rescue, youth coaches (all sports)
* Do a soup kitchen/ food pantry project once a week. Work with Salvation Army, Red Cross.
* Sponsor a warm coat/ mitten project for kids. Have a blanket distribution
* Have a "tea" for different groups. Honor students, exchange students, foreign students
* Honor someone each year like an outstanding citizen award.
* Group volunteer at rehab center, children's ward at hospital, pediatric center.
* Sponsor a flower show, art show, chalk on sidewalk art contest for kids, trash can decorating, Christmas decoration contest.
* Sponsor an Ice or Snow Sculpture contest for kids. Some places have Winter Fests. Provide speakers for Rotary, Kiwanis, Jaycees, Womens' Clubs fraternal organizations.
* Sponsor an old fashioned quilting party. Make quilt for needy family (s).
* Sponsor a "Mitten-knitting' project. Donate yarn, distribute mittens.

* Adopt a homeless shelter one day a week. Food Pantry, Soup kitchen or sandwiches
* Start a "mentor" program for unwed mothers, new mom's, newly married.
* Mentor kids of the incarcerated (check with prison officials). Adopt a family of deceased veteran, fire fighter, police officer. Adopt a handicapped veteran.
* Sponsor a literacy volunteer day at the library, youth center etc.
* Have a Walk "Walkie-Talkie" club—walk somewhere, have coffee, walk back.
* A Community meal once a week. (No charge, donations only everyone welcome.)

## Holiday Support Group

Holidays are the most difficult time of the year for grieving people. In many areas the holiday memorial service is a way to help people cope with the loneliness of the season. Try to get people out of the house and doing something meaningful.

A Christmas tree decorating ceremony for families who have experienced the death of a loved one within the last couple of years works very well. Each person places one ornament on the tree and briefly tells (or reads) something they will always remember about the person they are remembering; usually a poem, a statement or special accomplishments.

People from your area may have lost a loved one from another area by death. They should be encouraged to attend also. If there are not going to be enough people to decorate a large tree, a small one in a dining room area, a church entry-way, an entry-way to a bank, insurance company or other business where people would see it and think ahead to another year.

A centerpiece type of arrangement could also be used in a restaurant or meeting place.

Mark each decoration with a small identification ribbon, **_not stickers_** that could cause the decoration to be broken. Log in and I/D each decoration. Give people a date to pick them up after the holidays. I would encourage plenty of publicity explaining the project ahead of time.

Some memorial services use decorative candles which are lighted in memory of the deceased persons. They are encouraged to keep the candle following the service. Family members are invited to say things about their loved one. Suggest a time limit for each person to speak or read what they want to. Today many funeral homes have this type of memorial service for families they serve. Don't let that prevent you from having one for everyone in your area. People will surprise you and attend both services.

Consider a 24 hour holiday hotline for a week or so during the Christmas season. Open it for anyone that just wants someone to talk to over a holiday. Have emergency numbers handy, including suicide and poison prevention hotline numbers.

**Great ways to help you get through the holidays**

**Visit a shut-in. Renew an acquaintance**
**Volunteer at a hospital, nursing home, soup kitchen, food pantry, senior center etc.**
**Take a friend to lunch, a play or show.**
**Invite family & friends to a time of sharing.**
**Heal a broken relationship**

**Do New And Different Things:**

**Make a new friend. Try a new hobby.**

Get involved in a church, club etc.
Learn to play a new musical instrument.
Buy yourself something "special".
Take a walk. Enjoy the fresh air.

Do something your loved one would have enjoyed doing.
Bake some cookies. Give them away.
Change your routine.
Do for yourself.

## Widower Support Group

From what I have observed over the years, men seem to have a much harder time grieving the death of a mate than women do. I've seen several cases, and probably you have too, where I felt a man actually died of a broken heart _shortly_ after the death of his wife.

Let me remind you again, not to try to mix men and women's support groups! Some men are suspicious and fearful of women! They don't want to be hassled and they do **_not_** want a domineering woman chasing them.

Men's groups are very difficult to start and more difficult to keep active. I honestly believe that some men enjoy wallowing around in their own self pity. The challenge is to keep them from isolating. Give them a reason to get out of bed in the morning. One of the best projects to begin with is to start a "helping hands" group that will do odd jobs for shut-ins, elderly, single women and anyone else who can't do minor jobs by themselves. Word of mouth will keep the men's group busy. (Widows groups may want to do something similar.)

Try to establish some kind of a mentoring project for teens, or even younger kids with your widower support group. The first time I saw old Joe he had just stepped out of his wood working shop surrounded by a dozen or so little boys, each clutching a brightly painted lawn decoration they had made under old Joe's supervision. That evening, at the Vacation Bible School program the little boys displayed their creations to their parents. I'll never forget the admiration those parents had for their kids that evening and for old Joe! Try and "plug" your widowers support group in to a youth center, "Y" model airplane club or with some kind of a place for a wood working shop or craft area. There are many things that older men could teach kids today that they don't even know about: whittling, sharpening a saw, making a bird house, metal work, leather work, fire building, reading a compass, working with ropes, on and on.

Don't overlook the Boy and Girl Scouting programs. Each merit badge requires someone to certify the kid has met the requirements. A perfect place for an older man to shine. Big Brother-Sister groups, or city or federal programs in your area. There's a possibility the government has some kind of rehab program for vets that your guys could get involved with. Is there a Veterans hospital nearby?

Most men like to play cards. Get your group to volunteer to play cards with patients at area nursing homes, or put a write-up in the local paper that your group will play cards with shut-ins one afternoon or evening a week. Get a few each day of the week to volunteer at an area soup kitchen or food pantry. They might even plant a garden for them as a group. Start a surrogate grandfather's club. This would best be served by a group doing projects or just being with kids one afternoon a week. Make sure they're all _group_ activities.

Many churches do this anyway today so I don't have to tell you to be sure all adults having contact with kids get a police clearance. You don't need the reputation of having child molesters or sex offenders in your group. These are great projects, beneficial to many, but be sure you and your volunteers are protected.

There are "Take A Kid Fishing" projects and all kinds of sports programs where extra volunteers would be welcomed. Check out community and "Y" programs. Many high schools today have greenhouses that aren't used year round. Gardening projects for kids is a natural for both older guys and kids. One town I know of has a club they call the "Green Thumb Gang". They get kids involved with volunteers in beautification projects at every entrance to town, in vacant lots, traffic circles, and they've even made beautiful small parks throughout the area.

There are several projects around where men take old toys, repair and paint them for the Salvation Army, or other worthwhile causes. Many of the projects suggested for widows are also perfect for widowers. With volunteers, different youth directors at area churches could expand their programs. There could also be kids tournaments like horse shoes, tennis, golf etc. where kids could use coaching, and mentoring at the same time. Some older guys know a lot about outdoor "stuff". Get a group of older kids and take 'em on a nature hike, geology hike or birding. Touch base with emergency preparedness people in your area to offer volunteers. The Civil Air Patrol has a group of volunteers that probably could stand re-enforcement.

**The Life Appreciation Dynamic:** Everyone is unique, and should be remembered for those things that make us that way. If someone was a devout Christian, they should be buried with their Bible in their hand. If a person was a fisherman, their fish pole should be standing by their casket.

Following one service, a man's three sons hopped in the back of their father's pickup truck and drove out of the cemetery to symbolize going fishing with their dad, as kids. A trucker took his last ride on the back of his flatbed. Fire fighters have ridden to their grave on the back of a fire engine. Dozens of bikers escorted one of their own to the cemetery. The family flower arrangement at the funeral of an avid bridge player displayed a perfect bridge hand. One florist created a beautiful model of a snowmobile for a man who had died while riding on his. The same florist created a beautiful horse shoe shaped arrangement for a horse woman. She also embellished several wildlife trophies belonging to an avid hunter with plants and growths she had collected in the woods.

A military funeral with the folding of the flag, the firing squad and taps is indeed a fitting tribute for any veteran that fought for our nation.

**Before any support group dissolves for a last time, I strongly suggest a Life Appreciation Service within the group for the loved ones of those in the grief recovery group. Invite everyone to display one significant item or memorabilia (a photo, poem, Scripture, trophy, etc.) and offer a tribute to the life of the one they are grieving. It may be the last chance the person gets to say the things they need to about (or to) the one that they love.** Eventually everyone gets the same chance to express themselves.

Using the above information as a guide, ask each person to develop a Life Appreciation Service for their loved one. Don't hurry about doing this. Be sure everything is all "talked out" first.

This will bring memories flooding to the front and allow the person to talk about things they might have done differently and *say the things they needed to say to their loved one, and about them.*

Encourage each one to write a statement about the deceased person and read it at this special service. The most important thing is to get them to say the things they didn't get a chance to say before. There's about a 99% chance they didn't get to do it at the funeral (or memorial service).

Here's something else. When you are asking them to write these things down ask each one to include the things they didn't get a chance to say <u>besides</u> I love you, and good bye.

This may be very difficult, but <u>keep coming</u> back to that point until they get these things out in the open and talk about them! They *may not be able* to complete their relationship with the deceased person.

www.ingramcontent.com/pod-product-compliance
Lightning Source LLC
Chambersburg PA
CBHW031147020426
42333CB00013B/543